How to Read the Bible with Understanding

Second Edition

Lane A. Burgland

CONCORDIA PUBLISHING HOUSE • SAINT LOUIS

Copyright © 2016 Concordia Publishing House
3558 S. Jefferson Ave., St. Louis, MO 63118-3968
1-800-325-3040 • www.cph.org

Written by Lane A. Burgland

Edited by Edward A. Engelbrecht

Originally published in 1998 as *Reading the Bible with Understanding*.

Manufactured in the United States of America

Library of Congress Cataloging-in-Publication Data

Burgland, Lane A.

[Reading the Bible with understanding]

How to read the Bible with understanding / Lane Burgland. -- Second Edition.

pages cm

Rev. ed. of: Reading the Bible with understanding. © 1998.

Includes index.

ISBN 978-0-7586-4698-9

1. Bible--Study and teaching. 2. Bible--Hermeneutics. 3. Bible--Criticism, interpretation, etc. I. Title.

BS600.3.B87 2015

220.601--dc23 2014002376

1 2 3 4 5 6 7 8 9 10 25 24 23 22 21 20 19 18 17 16

Contents

Preface to the Second Edition

GENESIS 11:1–9 RECORDS HUMANITY'S EFFORTS TO DEFY THE will of God. They wanted to stay in the plain of Shinar rather than spread out over the face of the earth and populate it (which the Lord had commanded in Genesis 1:28 to Adam and Eve and repeated in Genesis 9:1 to Noah and his family). God, however, was serious about His command to populate the whole globe. He confused the single language used by all human beings up to that point. Unable to communicate, people spread out over the whole earth (Genesis 11:9).

In a way, we might say that the confusion of languages did not end in Genesis 11. It was merely the beginning. Languages, like the children of Adam and Eve, are born, grow, change, and finally die. We even refer to "living languages" and call languages that are no longer spoken "dead languages." Since languages change, new translations must be developed to communicate the Word of God in its truth and beauty. This is no easy task.

Efforts to produce a readable, accurate translation in English still continue today. In the 1990s, a group of scholars set out to develop a new translation using more of a "literal" approach to the text. This became the English Standard Version (ESV), which most recently underwent revisions in 2011. This second edition of *How to Read the Bible with Understanding* reflects the growing popularity of the ESV in many church bodies and includes a fuller discussion of modern translations and the challenges faced by translators.

We include a look at "The Friend at Midnight," a parable Jesus told to explain why God answers our prayers (Luke 11:5–8). The parable challenges translators and readers and lets us show how to use a number of the principles described in this book.

We also include in this edition a short survey of the history of biblical interpretation. Others before us have opened the Holy Scriptures and read and interpreted the Word of God. We can benefit from their experience and, perhaps, see the text from a slightly different perspective. Not only does each text have a context but so does each reader. Recognizing what impact a previous interpreter's culture and beliefs has on his or her reading of the Bible can help us become sensitive to the role our own context has on our interpretation.

Finally, we add a checklist for each reader to consider when opening Holy Scripture and beginning the wonderful, exciting, and challenging task of reading the Bible with understanding. May the Lord guide us each step of the way!

Lane A. Burgland
Churubusco, Indiana

The Commission on Theology and Church Relations of the Lutheran Church—Missouri Synod, in pursuing the assignment given by 2010 Synod Convention Resolution 3-07 To Prepare New Studies on Biblical Interpretation, reviewed this book and found it to be a helpful resource and guide to the interpretation of Scripture. The Commission encourages its use both for individual readers of the Scriptures and as a series of studies for group discussion. Additional resources deemed helpful by the Commission can be found at its website. Visit www.lcms.org/ctcr and explore the reports on Scripture found under "Resources."

INTRODUCTION

TALKING . . . LISTENING . . . WRITING . . . READING. EACH requires a unique set of skills. When we listen to someone who is speaking to us in person, we receive all sorts of clues to help us figure out what the other person means. Speakers use gestures, tone of voice, and rate of delivery to communicate their message. We see body language and hear changes in a person's delivery.

The processes for writing and reading are different. We see and hear none of these clues when we read what someone has written. Therefore a writer must use care and planning when putting thoughts down on paper in order to communicate the intended meaning. A reader, too, carefully reads and reflects on a text to interpret and understand what an author means.

In a way, reading the Bible is like reading any other book (or collection of books). A person reads a series of words that make up sentences and paragraphs and seeks to comprehend what is read. As literature or as history, the Bible is an open book. Anyone can read what is written (assuming it is translated well enough) and get the facts of the story—who did what to whom, where and when it occurred. The difficulty comes when we ask, "So what does it mean for us?"

Sometimes we hear people say that one person's interpretation is just as good as another's, or that any individual's understanding of a Bible passage is valid for that person. Our own experience should tell us that this is not true. When we write a letter to someone, we have a purpose in writing and want our reader to understand what we say. We write as clearly as possible, choosing the right words for our purpose, so that our reader doesn't misunderstand us.

God does the same thing with the Bible. Over a period of many centuries, through a variety of human authors, God has communicated His message. He wants us to understand both the facts of the story and His purpose in writing. (See John 20:30–31.) Reading the Bible with understanding means that we do not seek to understand merely the history of God's people or the story line of great literature. We read the Bible to understand what God says to us. We ask, "What does this mean?" and "What does this mean for me?" At this point, the Holy Spirit's guidance is essential.

Our own sinful nature blinds us to the Good News of Jesus Christ. (See Paul's comments in 2 Corinthians 4:3–4.) Reading the Bible is thus not only an intellectual exercise, but a spiritual battle.

The story of a blind man in John 9 parallels our reading of the Bible. Jesus healed that blind man. Later, when Jesus revealed Himself to that man, the formerly blind man saw his Savior and his Lord. He believed in Jesus and worshiped Him (John 9:38). The Pharisees in the story saw the same Jesus as did the blind man. Yet, in unbelief, they saw Jesus as an enemy of God and the Law. Both the formerly blind man and the Pharisees looked at the same man, but they came away with vastly different understandings. Were both "interpretations" of Jesus valid? Not at all! The blind man came away with true spiritual sight, the forgiveness of sins, and salvation. The Pharisees went away spiritually blind, condemned in their sin (John 9:41). The eternal destiny of all of these people rested on whether or not they understood who Jesus is—Son of God and Savior of the world.

In a similar way, what do people see when they read the Bible? Do they see a historical book of literature, or do they see the living Word of God (Hebrews 4:12)? As previously stated, reading the Bible does have much in common with reading any other book or letter. Its meaning is plain to anyone who reads it with an open mind. At the same time, reading the Bible is a unique experience; the Holy Spirit shows us our Savior in this book.

Reading the Bible is primarily the pursuit of the person who knows Jesus Christ as Savior and Lord and who wants to be "complete, equipped for every good work" (as Paul says of Scripture in 2 Timothy 3:17).

When we pick up the Bible, we should be honest with ourselves. We already have some ideas about what the Bible is all about and how to go about reading it. Everybody does. These become the principles we follow when we interpret the Bible. But are they the right ones?

Working through This Book

In part one, we will examine seven principles of interpretation and illustrate how they work for us. These rules are based on claims the Bible makes about itself, and they are confirmed by our own experiences as we read what other people write to us. The principles have been developed over the years to help us grasp what the author(s) meant. The principles are arranged from those that apply to most any type of book to those principles of climactic importance for reading and applying the Bible. The passages from the Bible for this first section will mostly be stories (prose or narrative), which are often easiest to explore first. In part one, we will also discuss the distinction between Law and Gospel, or between sin and grace, long recognized as an essential tool for reading the Bible.

Part two will concentrate on more difficult passages in the Bible. We will examine literary categories such as poetry, prophecy, parables, and apocalyptic writing (such as Revelation). Study of some passages will require the use of Bible dictionaries and encyclopedias. You will receive some hands-on experience with those tools.

In part three, we will give you some information about the Bible: who wrote the various books, when they were written, and how we got our English Bible, plus we'll give a quick evaluation of various Bible translations and paraphrases.

A number of good translations are available. The English Standard Version (ESV), New American Standard Bible (NASB), New Revised Standard Version (NRSV), the New King James Version (NKJV), and the New International Version (NIV) are all popular. We will trace the history of these translations in chapter 15. For the purposes of this book, we will use the ESV translation.

Since the Bible is a collection of sixty-six books, finding your way around in it can be somewhat of a challenge. Use your Bible's table of contents as a resource and a guide. Some people can look up passages by book, chapter, and verse very quickly. They have spent years acquiring that skill, so don't become discouraged if it takes you a while to find a particular section of the Bible.

In part four, we try to put it all together, offering some examples of tackling controversial or misunderstood topics and reading what Scripture really has to say about them. We try to give you a few pointers if you find yourself tasked with leading a Bible class. We encourage you to "follow your nose," reading with your curiosity turned on. Follow interesting leads and see where they take you. We include a history of interpretation as well as a checklist to use when reading the Scripture.

May God bless you as you begin your study of His Word!

Part One
Principles of Interpretation

The Bible was written many centuries ago in a setting far different from our own. Therefore a student of the Bible might ask, "How can I understand what the Bible is saying? The people, the cultures, and the languages are from a different age, and I am living in a modern age. Furthermore, I am not a theologian. I haven't gone to a seminary. Who will explain the meaning of the Bible to me?"

These seeming barriers are really no barriers at all. With the aid of the Holy Spirit, the student discovers that certain "keys" can help one understand the Bible and open its timeless truths. These keys, known also as principles of interpretation, are contained within the Bible itself. Thus, the Bible presents itself as an open book, with treasured meanings that can be understood by any Christian serious enough to seek God's message of salvation.

The principles in this text fall under the umbrella of three overriding beliefs:

- Scripture alone is the authority for Christian doctrine and practice, not human reason.
- We are saved only by God's grace (His undeserved love).
- We receive God's grace only through faith in Jesus Christ.

The more we read the Bible, the clearer it becomes that these three beliefs are drawn from Scripture itself.

Also, how often do conflicts arise because friends misunderstand messages they send, including oral communication? If "here and now" communication must overcome obstacles, we certainly need the help of the Holy Spirit to understand the "then and there" communication of Scripture. What did the original speaker or author mean, and what did the original hearer or reader understand when the message was first spoken or written? Chapter 7 will address this issue.

Chapter 1

Pay Attention to the Context

Whoever takes another meaning out of Scripture than the writer intended, goes astray. . . . The most skillful interpreter of the sacred writings, then, will be he who in the first place has read them all and retained them in his knowledge, if not yet with full understanding.

—Augustine[1]

Defining the Principle

WHAT DO YOU DO WHEN YOU PUT A JIGSAW PUZZLE TOGETHER? You probably look at the picture on the box. You have a better chance of getting the right piece in the right place if you can see the big picture. So it is with Scripture. We explain the parts in light of the whole. We recognize that the largest literary picture is the whole of the Bible.

The next smaller unit is the writing of a single author or a single book. (Some authors, like James, have only one book in the Bible; others, like Paul, have thirteen![2]) The next smaller context is the paragraph, although some literary units in Scripture are somewhat larger than this. When pastors are trained to examine the context, they often are warned that "a text without a context is a pretext." In other words, if you don't know the context of a passage, you will likely misinterpret it. People can make the Bible say almost anything they want it to say if they quote a passage out of context. Even Peter recognizes this. Writing about Paul's letters, Peter says, "There are some things in them that are hard to understand, which the ignorant and unstable twist to their own destruction, as they do the other Scriptures" (2 Peter 3:16b).

In this chapter, we will learn about five specific passages of Scripture and how their context helps us understand them. We will also take note of how their particular messages fit within the broad message that God communicates to us through the Scriptures.

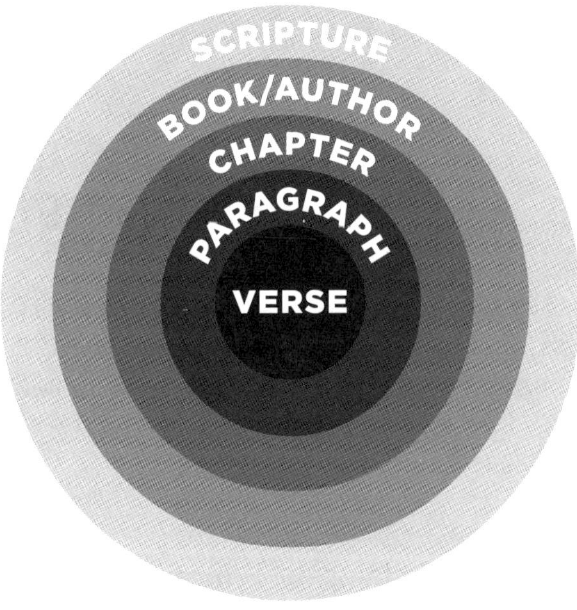

Applying the Principle

Romans 3:28

For our first example of precisely this point, let's take a look at Romans 3:28. There, Paul writes: "For we hold that one is justified by faith apart from works of the law." Based on Romans 3:21–31, answer the following questions:

1. What is the righteousness of God?
2. How much of the human race has sinned and fallen short of the glory of God?
3. How much of the human race has been justified by Jesus' death and resurrection?

4. What problem did the cross of Christ solve?
5. Since God is one, how many plans of salvation would He have?

In this passage, Paul uses a number of words that we don't often use. As a result, we may not clearly understand what he means when he uses them. For example, the word *righteousness* is an abstract noun that means the quality of being right or of doing the right thing. When used as an adjective in Scripture, it refers to the man or woman who keeps the entire Law of God. Ezekiel describes what it means to be righteous in 18:5–9.

When used to describe God, *righteous* means that God always keeps His Word. God does what He says He is going to do. Yet when we read the Old Testament, we might think that God sometimes breaks His Word. We read in Genesis 2 that God permitted Adam to eat from all the trees in the Garden of Eden except for the tree of the knowledge of good and evil, "for in the day that you eat of it you shall surely die" (v. 17).

In Genesis 3:1–6, the serpent contradicts God, claiming that Adam and Eve will not die if they eat from the tree. Eve chooses to doubt God's warning, eats from the tree, and does not drop dead. Adam is with her, watching, and when she does not drop dead he, too, eats from the fruit of the tree. He does not drop dead either. Even after God confronts them in Genesis 3, they do not appear to die. In fact, Adam lived 930 years before death claimed him (Genesis 5:5)!

In light of these events, can God be charged with unrighteousness? That is, can He be charged with failing to keep His Word? And what of all the other sins that seemingly went unpunished from the time of Adam to Christ? Paul refers specifically to this point when he writes that God punishes all sins in the person of Jesus Christ on the cross, demonstrating His righteousness (sometimes translated "justice"). In the cross of Christ, we see God's righteousness, for in the cross of Christ He punishes all sins, even those of Adam and Eve.

It is in the cross of Christ that we also see God's grace, freely justifying sinners through faith in Jesus. Note that *justify* means "to declare righteous." This is more than merely declaring someone innocent or not guilty. In Christ crucified, God declares us righteous. He gives us credit for fulfilling the Law in every respect and for never violating it (see Ezekiel 18:5–9). God places our sins upon Christ and, through faith in Jesus, credits us with having kept the entire Law. Therefore Paul writes in Romans 3:28, "For we hold that one is justified by faith apart from works of the law."

James 2:24

If what Paul writes in Romans 3 is right, then how can James say: "You see that a person is justified by works and not by faith alone" (James 2:24)? The answer lies in the different contexts of Romans 3 and James 2 and in the way each writer uses the verb *justify*.

First, we need to establish just what James is saying in his context. James is showing the connection between a living faith in Jesus Christ and the works that a Christian with such faith does. James emphasizes the external evidence of the internal faith so much so that he can define true religion as taking care of widows and orphans in their distress and in avoiding the immorality of the world (James 1:27). The good deeds done by believers show their faith to the world. Where there are no good deeds, there is no faith. Where there is faith, there are good deeds (acts of compassion and kindness, especially to fellow Christians; see James 2:14–17).

What role do these good deeds play in someone's salvation? They are the evidence of faith. As such, they serve as a legal exhibit on the Last Day. On that day of final judgment, when Jesus judges the living and the dead, He will point to these compassionate applications of saving faith as evidence for a person's eternal destiny.

Jesus presents this same picture in the story of the sheep and the goats (Matthew 25:31–46). God separates the sheep and goats before He describes their deeds. Their eternal destiny is already known. The sheep receive their inheritance—eternal life—through their faith in Jesus, which they demonstrated through acts of caring. The goats, on the other hand, receive their eternal punishment because they do not have faith in Jesus. God does not proclaim great evil in their lives, but their lives reflect no saving faith in any acts of compassion done to Jesus' followers. If the word *justify* can refer to this public proclamation of judgment, then we can understand how James can say that "a person is justified by works and not by faith alone" (James 2:24).

In contrast with the context in James, Paul seeks to make a different point while using some of the same words. When Paul uses the verb *justify*, he refers to God's declaration that all people are righteous (Romans 3:23–24) through the sacrifice of Christ Jesus. Paul also uses the word *justify* to refer to that moment when an individual is declared right with God through faith in Jesus (Romans 3:26, 28). Paul refers to what we term *justification*, and James refers to that public proclamation of judgment that is based on what we call *sanctification*. If we misunderstand Paul in Romans 3:28, we might think that we can live our lives in an immoral or selfish way and it would make no difference. If we misunderstand James in James 2:24, we might think that we are partially or entirely responsible for our own salvation because of our good works. Reading Paul and James in the light of their contexts (Romans 3:21–31; James 2:14–26), we realize that they are emphasizing two different parts of the Christian's life with God, both of which are important.

Matthew 19

Look next at the importance of context in Matthew 19. Read Matthew 19:16–28 and answer the following questions:

1. How does someone enter eternal life according to Jesus in verse 17?
2. What does it take to be a perfect disciple of Jesus according to Jesus in verse 21?
3. Under the theory that God loves rich people the most (because He has given them the most material blessings), a rich man is the "most likely to succeed" when it comes to entering the kingdom of God. What does Jesus say about the chances that even the best of us can earn our way into the Kingdom according to verse 24?
4. How do the disciples respond to Jesus' statement in verse 24? (See v. 25.)
5. What does Jesus then say in verse 26 about any person's chances of earning eternal life?

If we take the question of the rich young man and Jesus' answer out of context, we might think that we have to keep all the commandments of God and sell everything and give our money to the poor in order to enter the kingdom of God and receive eternal life. After all, that's exactly what Jesus says in verses 17 and 21. However, this teaching directly contradicts other passages of Scripture where we learn that we are saved by faith in Jesus Christ alone (as is clearly taught in Romans 3:28 and Ephesians 2:8–9). So how should we understand the responses of Jesus in Matthew 19:17 and 21?

The rich young man believes that he can do good works and thus earn God's approval. However, he has not been able to achieve peace with God by this method. He thinks he has fulfilled all the commandments, but he still searches for assurance of salvation. He comes to Jesus in the hope of finding that assurance and peace.

The Pharisees in Matthew 19:1–12 also have come to Jesus with a question, but they are not seeking peace. They hope to trap Jesus in a difficult question, in the same geographical area where John the Baptist was arrested for criticizing the marriage of Herod Antipas to his sister-in-law, Herodias. John lost his head, and perhaps the Pharisees want Jesus to get into the same trouble!

These two stories have something important in common. Both the rich young man and the Pharisees share a common assumption: you can earn God's approval. The Pharisees believe that Deuteronomy 24:1–4 permitted divorce under some circumstances and debated what those circumstances were. However, Jesus reminds them that God's original plan had been that a man and woman marry and stay married all their lives together. Jesus does something quite similar with the rich young man. By answering as He does, He confronts the rich young man with the impossibility of fulfilling the Law, just as the Pharisees were confronted with their own opposition to God's plan in Matthew 19:1–12.

The Pharisees go away frustrated and the rich young man goes away disappointed, because Jesus used the Law as a mirror to cause them to see themselves clearly, to show them that their whole way of thinking was wrong. Nobody enters the kingdom of God because he or she has earned God's stamp of approval. Jesus agrees with the disciples that it is absolutely impossible for us to save ourselves from God's wrath on Judgment Day (19:26). But Jesus does not stop with the words, "With man this is impossible." He adds, "But with God, all things are possible." This, then, is the key to the chapter. Sandwiched between the story of the Pharisees with their question about divorce and the story of the rich young man with his question about earning eternal life, we find a short story that may at first seem out of place. In Matthew 19:13–15, Jesus receives little children and says that "to such belongs the kingdom of heaven." With that, He places His hands on them and blesses them.

God's approval comes not through keeping the commandments or even selling all we have and giving our money to the poor. God's approval, and thus eternal life, comes through Jesus Christ. He receives those who trust in Him, blesses them, and brings them into the kingdom of God. Jesus' disciples were shocked by His answer to the Pharisees (19:10) and panicked by His conversation with the rich young man (19:27). They even tried to prevent the little children from reaching Jesus (19:13). In short, they did not understand that human beings have no hope of earning eternal life by their good works.

Matthew writes these three stories so that we, the readers of his Gospel, might understand what the disciples failed to understand. The context of the chapter makes it clear why Jesus tells the rich young man what He does in 19:17: Jesus shows him the Law with its impossible demands in order to drive him to the Gospel of full and free acceptance by grace through faith in Jesus Christ.

Mark 4:10–12 and Isaiah 6:9

In the first part of this chapter, we saw how some writers use the same words with slightly different meanings (James 2:24 and Romans 3:28) and how the whole of Scripture provides a "safety net" for interpreting those passages. In the second part (Matthew 19), we saw how the entire chapter helps us understand a particular verse. In the third and final part of this chapter, we will see that checking out the Old Testament context when the New Testament quotes it will help us understand the meaning of the verse. We will look at Mark 4:12, where Jesus speaks of His reason for using parables, and consider the context of the Old Testament citation—Isaiah 6:9.

Read Mark 4:10–12 and answer the following questions:

1. Who or what does Jesus call "the secret of the kingdom of God"?
2. Why does Jesus teach in parables?
3. What Old Testament passage does Jesus quote?

The first extended parable of Jesus appears in Mark 4 (parallel passages are Matthew 13:1–15 and Luke 8:4–10). It seems that Jesus did not use parables (or at least none are recorded) in the early months of His ministry. Only after opposition developed did Jesus begin to use parables. (See Mark 3:6 where the Pharisees and Herodians plot together to kill Him.) This provides the background for Jesus' statement in 4:11–12.

Two groups of people spend time near Jesus—His disciples and His enemies. To the disciples, Jesus explains what the parables mean. To them, He reveals the "secrets" of the kingdom of God—that He is the Messiah who has come to give His life on the cross as a ransom for all people. Jesus' enemies are waiting for Him to say something so that they may charge Him in court with a crime, preferably a capital crime. When Jesus teaches the Good News, that He is the promised Messiah, He does so covertly so that these enemies have no ammunition to use against Him in a religious or criminal court of law. In other words, because Jesus' enemies have hardened themselves against Him, He uses parables.

The Old Testament passage He cites in support of this approach is Isaiah 6:9. This verse comes from the section where Isaiah receives his call to be a prophet from God. God warns him that the people of Israel will not listen to his message or respond to his call for repentance, for they have hardened themselves against God and His Word. The preaching of God's Word, both Law and Gospel, will have the same effect on these people of Isaiah's day as it did on many in Jesus' day—it will make their minds even more closed to God's message. They have chosen this path; it is nobody's fault but their own. The key question for Isaiah to ask is simply, "How long, O Lord?" (Isaiah 6:11).

God answers Isaiah's question by noting that this hardening is temporary, and that after the Assyrians have devastated Israel and the Babylonians have led Judah away into captivity, He will continue to keep His promise to send a Savior, the Messiah (Isaiah 6:11–13). Here, we also have a key to interpreting Mark 4:12.

Jesus will advance to the cross. Using the opposition of His enemies, He will see to it that He is crucified according to the timetable He established before the foundation of the world. It would not do for Him to be rushed to the cross prematurely, before He finished the work the Father sent Him to do in His earthly ministry. By teaching in "code"—that is, by using parables—Jesus retains control of the situation and control of His destiny. When that destiny is accomplished—when He has given His life as the sacrifice for the sins of the world—then the "secrets" of the kingdom of God will be proclaimed openly for all people to see and perceive, hear and understand. In short, the hardening of His larger audience is temporary.

The context of Mark 4 confirms this interpretation. In verse 22, Jesus says, "For nothing is hidden except to be made manifest; nor is anything secret except to come to light." In both Mark 4:9 (which sets up the quote from Isaiah) and in Mark 4:23 (which marks the end of a literary unit that began at 4:9), Jesus says, "He who has ears to hear, let him hear." Scripture clearly teaches that God "desires all people to be saved and to come to the knowledge of the truth" (1 Timothy 2:4).When Christ dies on the cross, He dies for all people (Romans 3:23–24). The fact that Jesus recognizes the hostility of His enemies and avoids their traps does not contradict His love for people, including those who oppose Him. Mark reminds us (in 4:12) that Jesus is master of the situation and that He can even use people who want to see Him dead to work out His plan of salvation.

A Key to Interpretation

We close this chapter with one more point: whenever we read Scripture and interpret it in a way that robs us of our assurance of God's love in Christ Jesus, or when we misunderstand a passage so that we lose the conviction that we are truly saved by grace through faith in Jesus Christ, we have gotten off on the wrong track. God gave us the Bible to lead us to faith in Jesus Christ and thus to have life in His name (John 20:30–31). Paying attention to this most important broad context as we interpret Scripture will help us to realize the joy of our salvation, which is so very precious to each of us.

Chapter 1 Notes

1. *On Christian Doctrine* 1.36.41, 2.8.12 (*Select Library of Nicene and Post-Nicene Fathers*).
2. Some suggest that Paul wrote fourteen, counting the Epistle to the Hebrews as his.

Chapter 2

Stick with the Plain and Obvious Meaning of a Text

The entire Scriptures, the prophets, and the Gospels, can be clearly, unambiguously, and harmoniously understood by all.

—Irenaeus of Lyons[1]

Defining the Principle

COMMUNICATION IS A DIFFICULT ART. WE CHOOSE OUR WORDS and we put them together in sentences, hoping the other person will understand what we are saying or writing. At times, though, we don't say what we mean or mean what we say. Sometimes we use irony or sarcasm to make our point, sometimes we exaggerate or use hyperbole for emphasis, and sometimes we use puns and wordplays for humorous effect.

The best rule of thumb when reading Scripture is to read it as straightforward communication unless the text contains some indicator that we should disregard the usual and customary meaning of the words or paragraphs.

Applying the Principle

Mark 5:21–43

Perhaps the best way to get a handle on this principle is to read Mark 5:21–43. We will then examine three additional passages to illustrate the principle.

Mark 5:21–43 is actually two stories, one set inside the other. They form the climax for a series of miracles that begins in 4:35 (Jesus calms the storm) and continues into chapter 5 (Jesus exorcises many demons from a man). By the end of chapter 5, the reader has seen Jesus command nature, give orders to a multitude of demons, heal the incurably sick with a touch of His garment, and raise the dead. We may summarize the account as follows.

In chapter 5, Mark shows us four scenes that clearly answer the question, "Who is Jesus?" The last two stories (a woman sick for twelve years and a twelve-year-old dead girl) focus especially on faith, trusting Jesus as Savior. Mark then contrasts the faith of the woman and the faith of the dead girl's parents with the unbelief of Jesus' hometown (Mark 6:1–6).

These stories about the woman and the girl also prepare the reader for chapter 7 where Jesus abolishes the distinction between "clean" and "unclean" (referring to the ceremonial status of food and people under the Mosaic Law). Since both the woman with the flow of blood and the dead girl would have been unclean under Mosaic Law (see Leviticus 15:25; Numbers 19:13), Jesus should have been rendered unclean by contact. If you touch something unclean (or it touches you), you are rendered unclean and must go through the purification process (Leviticus 5:2–3, 6). In fact, He remained ceremonially clean as healing and life flowed from Him to the woman and the girl. This would set the stage for outreach to the formerly unclean Gentiles (reaffirmed in Acts 10:1–11:18), a crucial point for the Early Church as well as the fundamental teaching of all Scripture that we are saved by grace through Jesus Christ alone. Who is Jesus that He can do these impossible things? Mark ultimately answers this question in Peter's confession ("You are the Christ," Mark 8:29) and the centurion's statement ("Truly this man was the Son of God," Mark 15:39).

With these broader points in view, we can now get focused. Applying the principle of interpretation for this chapter of our study, does anything in Mark 5:21–43 require us to understand these two stories in a nonliteral sense? In other words, does Mark indicate in the text that we should take these two stories as a metaphor or in a figurative way? If not, then we can conclude that Mark thought of these stories as actual events in real history. He presents them to us as a straightforward account of what really occurred when a sick woman interrupted Jesus' journey to help a dying girl.

Some people believe that miracles can't happen. They work on the principle that "if I haven't seen it, it can't be true." They read these stories about Jesus and try to draw some "spiritual truth" from what they consider to be a myth. However, without the miraculous nature of these healings, we lose Mark's whole point. Mark wants to show the reader that Jesus is the Christ (Mark 8:29), the Son of God (Mark 15:39).

In order to show us that we can trust Jesus as the woman and the girl's parents trusted Jesus, these events really had to happen (which is how Mark presents them). Otherwise, we would have to say that Mark was asking us to trust in someone who couldn't help us by telling us things that never happened. Yet Mark also does not record these events as a promise that faith in Jesus will cure *all* disease and prevent physical death. These sad events happen to Christians all the time.

Rather, Mark's point is this: Jesus has power over nature and demons, over sickness and death. The Holy Spirit, by recording these miracles, invites us to trust in Jesus for rescue from our biggest problem: sin and the righteous wrath of God against sinners. Salvation comes to the hopelessly unclean through faith in Jesus of Nazareth.

Some people have a worldview that excludes the possibility of the supernatural. Others believe no divine intervention is possible in the daily affairs of the world. When these people read the miracle stories in the Bible, they cannot accept them at face value. These Bible readers are bound to misunderstand Scripture. The authors of Scripture (Mark included) present the miracles as fact. Since nothing in the context compels us to understand the words in some other way, we, too, take these words of Scripture in the normal, intended sense—as fact.

Matthew 28:1–10

We look next at Matthew 28:1–10, where Matthew records the resurrection of Jesus. Based on the story in this section, answer the following:

1. What day of the week is it?
2. Who goes to the tomb of Jesus?

3. Who comes to the tomb ahead of them?
4. What unusual events accompany this first visitor?
5. What message does the visitor have?
6. Whom do these women meet on the way back to the disciples?
7. Why is the women's fear turned into joy?
8. Where is the body of Jesus?
9. How does your answer to the previous question affect your expectation, if any, for your own physical resurrection on Judgment Day?

An angel came to Jesus' tomb, rolled the stone back, and announced that Jesus had risen from the dead. The women ran away from the tomb, but on the way to the disciples they met Jesus, who spoke to them. The story is straightforward, narrated as factual history. The text contains no indication that anything is to be taken figuratively or symbolically. The problem for the modern reader does not lie in what the text says, but in whether he or she believes that the Bible is absolutely true. If you believe that it is true, you accept as truth that angels exist and you believe in the possibility of a physical resurrection from the dead. These beliefs have a profound impact on how you interpret and understand the story.

Matthew 26:17–35

Human reason can be a valuable tool in Bible study. We use our human reason and study skills to explore the text. However, the use of reason has its limits. It must remain subject to God's Word. Thus, we do not place ourselves above the text. Rather, we place ourselves under the Scripture, relying on the power of the Holy Spirit to create, sustain, and build our faith, and we use human reason only to help understand the intended meaning. Note how the use of reason affects the interpretation of Matthew 26:17–35. Answer the following questions:

1. During which Jewish festival does Jesus eat the Last Supper?
2. What importance did it have for the Jews? You may want to read Exodus 11–13 for more background. Why is it helpful to know this?
3. What does Jesus say when He gives His disciples the bread?
4. What does Jesus say when He gives His disciples the wine?

5. Can we humanly comprehend the text? Should we explain what we don't understand in human terms?

In this account of the Last Supper, Jesus says, "Take, eat; this is My body" (v. 26). He also says, "This is My blood of the covenant, which is poured out for many for the forgiveness of sins" (v. 28). The words are plain enough, but what do they mean? Is there any reason to believe that they mean something different? If we come to the text with open minds, we see that Jesus means what He says, "This is My body . . . this is My blood of the covenant."

Sometimes we use the word *is* to mean "represents." We might hold up a picture of a child and say: "This is my daughter." What we mean, of course, is "This is a picture of my daughter." In a way, the picture represents the person who is in it. We are able to figure out the meaning of the word *is* by context. If someone holds up a picture, we have no problem understanding what is meant because the photograph or painting is right in front of us. But what if we are on the other side of a door when we hear someone say, "This is my daughter"? We can't see if that person is pointing to an individual or to a photograph. Quite naturally, we would assume the person is referring to his actual daughter.

When we read in Matthew's Gospel that Jesus said, "This is My body," we have to determine what He meant by *this*. From the immediate context, it is clear that *this* refers to the bread. Further, since the text does not provide any clues that Jesus means something other than the plain meaning of the words, we should take the Words of Institution to mean that Jesus offers His body in, with, and under the bread He gives to His disciples.

We do not know how this happens or even how this is possible. These simply are the words Matthew wrote. He provides no textual clues to indicate that we should take it any other way. Our human reason might argue that such a miracle is not possible because we can't do it ourselves. But remember, Jesus' miraculous power surpasses our ability to understand it. Therefore, we let Scripture be the authority and the human mind be its servant.

How can readers check their understanding of a text—apply, as it were, a kind of quality control? After reading a passage and drawing a conclusion about its meaning, we might ask, "What if the writer had said it differently?" This question assumes that the Holy Spirit inspired the various authors of Scripture to write in the clearest manner possible, expressing the intended meaning as plainly as they could. Each word, each sentence, then, becomes integral to the meaning of a verse or text.

Matthew 28:16–20

Take, for example, the Great Commission in Matthew 28:16–20. Answer the following questions:

1. Where and when did Jesus give the Great Commission?
2. With what authority does Jesus give this commission?
3. To whom does Jesus give this commission?
4. How are Jesus' followers to make other disciples?
5. What does Jesus promise at the end?

Here, Jesus commissions His *listeners* to "make disciples of all nations" by baptizing them in the name of the triune God and by teaching them to obey everything He has commanded His disciples. Jesus meant what He said—all nations—which include people of all races, ages, and personalities.

Jesus makes no distinctions based on age, sex, ethnic background, or other such things. Sent by the Father, Jesus sends His disciples out into the world to make more disciples. He directs them to do this by baptizing and by teaching. If we have previously made up our minds that infants should not be baptized, we will not understand the Great Commission as Jesus intended it. Once again, the difficulty in interpreting a text often lies not in the words, but in the attitudes and ideas of the reader.

All of us have opinions and beliefs about God, Jesus, and what is going on in the Bible. Sometimes those get in the way of understanding a text as its author intended. As hard as it is to do, we have a better chance of getting the point of a passage if we keep our minds as open as possible and pay attention to what the author actually writes in the section we are studying.

Finally, the Bible should make sense. Its content was written for the purpose of being read and for leading the reader to Jesus Christ as Savior and Lord, as John says in John 20:30–31. God inspired men to write the book in the language of the people so that ordinary, common people would see and believe in Jesus. Except for a few sections where God apparently chose to communicate in a unique way for a specific reason (like parts of Zechariah, Ezekiel, Daniel, and Revelation), the Bible is not written in some code that requires experts to explain it to the rest of us.

The message of the Bible is, in many ways, a simple message of sin and grace, Law and Gospel, written so that the average person can understand. Jesus Himself says, "I thank You, Father, Lord of heaven and earth, that You have hidden these things from the wise and understanding and revealed them to little children" (Matthew 11:25). Thus, the second principle of biblical interpretation is *stick to the plain and obvious meaning of the text.*

Chapter 2 Note

1. *Against Heresies*, Book II, XXVII, 2.

Chapter 3

Scripture Interprets Scripture

> *The safest of all ways to search for the meaning of Scripture is to strive for it by a comparison of passages and by observation.*
>
> —Martin Luther[1]

Defining the Principle

"MEASURE TWICE AND CUT ONCE." THIS ADVICE, GIVEN BY older carpenters to younger apprentices, helps the Bible student as well. We want to make sure we have the right understanding of a particular passage, so we check our understanding of it against another similar passage ("measure twice"). We might also think of this third principle as a type of quality control, where we see if we have the right understanding.

Applying the Principle

1 Corinthians 15

In chapter 2, we read about the resurrection of Jesus (Matthew 28:1–10). The plain meaning of the text was that Jesus physically rose from the dead on the third day after His death and burial. To check our understanding, we turn to 1 Corinthians 15. Throughout this long chapter (fifty-eight verses), Paul writes about the resurrection of Jesus and what it means. Based on verses 1–8, answer the following questions:

1. What is the heart of the Gospel (mentioned in vv. 1 and 2)? (See vv. 3 and 4 for the answer.)
2. What does Paul mean by the phrase "in accordance with the Scriptures" (vv. 3–4)?
3. How does Paul confirm the physical resurrection of Jesus to his readers? (See vv. 5–7.)

When you answer the second question, it may be helpful to read some of the introduction to 1 Corinthians in a study Bible to learn about the historical context. Paul probably wrote 1 Corinthians in AD 55, before the Gospels of Matthew, Mark, Luke, and John were widely circulated. This helps us understand the phrase "in accordance with the Scriptures" as a reference to Old Testament prophecy. Thus, Paul tells us that the death and resurrection of Jesus were prophesied in the Old Testament. Paul confirms the physical resurrection of Jesus by

- affirming this is what he was told (15:3–4);
- listing eyewitnesses (15:5–8);
- pointing out the consequences if Jesus had not been raised (15:12–19); and
- pointing out the consequences of Jesus' resurrection (15:20–24).

1 Corinthians 11–14

Using Scripture to interpret Scripture helps us understand the Lord's Supper as well. In chapter 2, we used Matthew 26:17–35 to illustrate interpretation based on the plain and obvious meaning of the text. We also find other Scripture to support that interpretation, in this case 1 Corinthians 11:17–34.

The Church at Corinth suffers from a number of problems, including conduct at worship services. Paul addresses these problems in 1 Corinthians 11:3–14:40. In 11:17–34, he speaks directly to their celebration of the Lord's Supper and outlines the problem in 11:17–22. Based on verses 17–34, answer the following questions:

1. How have divisions within the congregation affected their celebration of the Lord's Supper?
2. Where does Paul begin when he addresses the issue (11:23–26)?

3. Against what does a person sin when taking the Lord's Supper unworthily?
4. Why are many Corinthian Christians sick and weak, and why have some "fallen asleep" (NIV)?
5. What things should a person do before taking the Lord's Supper?

Paul recognized the many divisions within the Corinthian Church in chapter 1 (vv. 10–17). He appealed to the members to heal their divisions and unite their minds and thoughts in Jesus Christ (v. 10). These divisions are connected with most of the problems Paul writes about in this letter, including their observance of the Lord's Supper. For various reasons (which Paul does not mention), members of the Corinthian Church arrive at their place of worship at different times. As strange as it seems, some of those who arrive early eat and drink the elements of the Lord's Supper, and as a result later arrivals don't get any and the early arrivals actually get drunk from drinking all the wine!

When Paul corrects the Corinthians, he makes a point of repeating the Words of Institution (11:23–25). Paul's understanding of the Lord's Supper is based on the words Jesus spoke when He handed the bread and wine to His disciples. This helps us check our interpretation of Matthew 26. Paul writes (in 1 Corinthians 11:27) that someone who eats the bread or drinks the cup of the Lord in an unworthy manner will be guilty of sinning against the body and blood of the Lord Jesus Christ, not merely of abusing bread and wine. Paul had already written about this connection between the body of Jesus and the bread, as well as the wine of the Lord's Supper and the blood of Jesus, in 10:16–22. He now specifically directs Christians to examine themselves before taking the Lord's Supper because the body and the blood of Jesus are really present with the bread and wine. Some Christians at Corinth have already suffered for their misuse of the Lord's Supper. Some have gotten sick, some have become weak, and some have "fallen asleep" (that is, died, as in the ESV). Paul adds that if these Christians had "judged" the Lord's Supper correctly, God would not have had to judge them by such severe discipline as sickness and death. Nevertheless, God did discipline them so that they would not be condemned on the Last Day (1 Corinthians 11:32). Like a loving Father, God loves with a "tough love" because the stakes are so high.

"Son of Man"

The third principle of interpretation, that Scripture interprets Scripture, has helped us check our understanding of the resurrection account in Matthew as well as his record of the Last Supper. We see another way Scripture interprets Scripture in Jesus' use of the phrase "Son of Man." In Mark's Gospel, Jesus uses it first in 2:10 and for the second time in 2:28. In the Old Testament, this phrase usually means "human being," as in Psalm 8:4. There, the psalmist sets "son of man" in the second line of the verse, parallel to "man" in the first line. The two terms are roughly equivalent in this psalm. Similarly, in Ezekiel God uses "son of man" to address the prophet (as in Ezekiel 2:1). The term emphasizes the humanity of the prophet, particularly in contrast to the divinity of God. But is that all Jesus means when He calls Himself the "Son of Man"?

The first time Jesus uses this phrase in Mark, He says, "But that you may know that the Son of Man has authority on earth to forgive sins . . ." (2:10). The second time Jesus calls Himself by the title, He says, "So the Son of Man is lord even of the Sabbath" (2:28). We can readily see that Jesus has more in mind than *Son of Man = human being* in these two verses! The power to forgive sins and the authority to judge what is and is not acceptable on the Sabbath ordinarily do not rest with man, but with God. As we read through Mark's Gospel, we eventually come to the key passage that helps us unlock what Jesus means by "Son of Man." In Mark 14:62, when the high priest asks Jesus directly if He is the Christ, "the Son of the Blessed" (that is, the Son of God), Jesus answers, "I am." And He adds, "And you will see the Son of Man seated at the right hand of Power, and coming with the clouds of heaven."

Jesus quotes Daniel 7:13–14, where the prophet sees a vision of the Last Day. On that day of universal judgment, the ultimate judge is described as "one like a son of man" who comes with the authority of God to judge all people of all nations and rule over an everlasting kingdom. By quoting this passage, Jesus reveals what He has in His mind when He says "Son of Man." Jesus declares Himself to be that divine judge of all people on the Last Day, the "ultimate referee" who has the authority to forgive sins or not to forgive. He has divine authority to decide what is right and wrong behavior on the Sabbath day. By allowing Scripture to interpret Scripture, we find that "Son of Man" means much more than merely human; it means that Jesus is the divine judge of all the living and the dead.

Chapter 3 Note

1. *What Luther Says* (St. Louis: Concordia, 1959), §297.

Chapter 4

Interpret Scripture in Light of the Rule of Faith

Receive, my children, the Rule of Faith. . . . These words which you have heard are in the Divine Scriptures . . . gathered and reduced into one.

—Augustine[1]

Defining the Principle

IN THE PREVIOUS CHAPTER, WE SAW HOW A RELATED PASsage can helpfully explain another. In this chapter, we encounter a similar principle. This new principle reflects the conviction that all sixty-six books of the Bible share a unity of belief and teaching without diminishing the individuality and distinctive contributions of each of those books and their authors.

Even though many different people wrote the Bible over a period of fifteen hundred years or so, the Bible is ultimately one Word of God. We properly distinguish different teachings in this Word, and we appreciate the diversity of material within this Word, but we also confess that the Bible possesses a fundamental "oneness." In this chapter, we will examine two places where New Testament authors cite the Old Testament, and then examine two New Testament doctrines (the way of salvation and the divinity of Jesus) where Scripture seems to say two opposite and contradictory things.

New Testament writers use the Old Testament in a variety of ways. Sometimes a New Testament writer merely *alludes* to an Old Testament text, referring to a person or an event without actually quoting the text. For example, Jesus refers to the time when David, on the run from King Saul, ate the consecrated bread at the tabernacle (1 Samuel 21:1–6). Jesus does not quote the Old Testament, but refers to the fact that David ate the forbidden bread out of necessity, confirming His point about what was legal or illegal on the Sabbath (Mark 2:23–28).

At other times, Jesus *quotes* the Old Testament. For example, when Satan tempted Jesus, Jesus cites Deuteronomy three times, treating Scripture as authoritative and as a powerful tool against the devil (Matthew 4:1–11 and Luke 4:1–13). Even Satan quotes Scripture in an effort to drive a wedge between the Father and the Son.

In one case, a New Testament author quotes another New Testament passage as authoritative Scripture. In 1 Timothy 5:18, Paul writes, "For the Scripture says, 'You shall not muzzle an ox when it treads out the grain,' and 'The laborer deserves his wages.'" The first quote is from Deuteronomy 25:4, but the second citation never appears in the Old Testament. It matches exactly, however, a statement of Jesus in Luke 10:7. Another New Testament author, Peter, refers to Paul's writings as Scripture (2 Peter 3:15–16). These two passages reflect the recognition by the Early Church of several New Testament writings as Holy Scripture, equal in authority and status to the Hebrew Scriptures. The apostles recognized and relied upon the oneness of Scriptural teaching, which the Early Christians summarized in the Apostles' Creed.

Applying the Principle

Isaiah 7:14

Sometimes the meaning of an Old Testament passage doesn't become clear until the New Testament uses it. See, for example, Isaiah 7:14, which Matthew quotes in 1:23. Following good practice, we look first at the original context of the Old Testament citation. Ahaz was king of Judah when the events of Isaiah 7 unfolded. Two kings to the north (Syria and Israel) formed an alliance against the nation of Assyria and wanted Judah to join them. When Ahaz refused, the two northern nations planned to invade Judah and establish their own puppet king. Isaiah reminded Ahaz of God's promise and warned against Ahaz inviting Assyria to help him out against the two northern kingdoms. Asked to pick a sign as confirmation of God's dependability, Ahaz refused. As a result, the Lord Himself chooses the sign: "The virgin shall conceive and bear a son, and shall call His name Immanuel" (Isaiah 7:14).

Over the years quite a lot of ink has been spilled over what this passage means. What did Isaiah mean by virgin? Who was this virgin? When did she or would she live? Not until the New Testament does the meaning become fully clear. When Matthew recounts the birth of Jesus, he quotes Isaiah 7:14. He tells us that Mary became pregnant before she had any sexual contact with a man (confirmed in Luke 1:34). Mary conceived Jesus by the power of the Holy Spirit (Matthew 1:18, 20; Luke 1:35) while still a virgin. Matthew then adds, "All this took place to fulfill what the Lord had spoken by the prophet: 'Behold, the virgin shall conceive and bear a son, and they shall call His name Immanuel' (which means God with us)" (Matthew 1:22–23).

We can summarize the sign the Holy Spirit gave to Ahaz through Isaiah almost eight hundred years earlier as follows: if you want a sign that points to God's salvation, look for the pregnant virgin. The virgin birth of Jesus fulfills the prophecy that God gave to Isaiah and that Isaiah then offered to Ahaz as proof of God's trustworthiness. God will rescue His people and preserve the Davidic line, from whom Ahaz is descended. Sadly, Ahaz rejected God's Word through Isaiah and sought an alliance with Assyria (2 Kings 16:5–18; 2 Chronicles 28:16–21).

What did Isaiah's prophecy mean for Ahaz? God promised that by the time the child Immanuel was old enough to "refuse the evil and choose the good" (Isaiah 7:15–16), Judah's enemies would be destroyed. As it turned out, within two or three years of the original prophecy of Isaiah 7:14 (735–734 BC), the Assyrians defeated Israel in battle and conquered Syria (2 Kings 15:29; 16:7–9). A few years after that, they conquered Israel as well (722 BC; see 2 Kings 17). How would God have dealt with these two northern nations had Ahaz believed the prophecy and not asked for help from Assyria? Only God Himself knows.

What did Isaiah's prophecy mean for Matthew? God promised to rescue His people from their sin (Matthew 1:21, a promise expressed in the name *Jesus*). When and where will God accomplish this rescue? When the virgin becomes with child and when she gives birth. Many people have come claiming to be God's Anointed One (*Messiah* from the Hebrew; *Christ* from the Greek), God's chosen instrument for deliverance and salvation. How are we supposed to know who is truly that Chosen One? Find the One who is born of a virgin, and you've found Him!

By looking at how a New Testament author handled a passage from the Old Testament, we see that Isaiah's prophecy finds its fulfillment in Jesus, conceived and born of a virgin, who has come so that He might save us from a peril far worse than an alliance of kings who want to wage war against us. He has come to save us from our sins. We can see in Isaiah's account and its fulfillment in Matthew the oneness of Holy Scripture.

Hosea 6:6

We can see how this principle works when Jesus quotes Hosea 6:6, as He does on two occasions: Matthew 9:13 and 12:7. In the original context, Hosea calls God's people to repentance. He reminds them that even an external observance of God's Law with its sacrifices and burnt offerings does not really describe the heart of the relationship between God and His people. Hosea writes: "For I desire steadfast love and not sacrifice, the knowledge of God rather than burnt offerings" (6:6). Based on this verse, answer the following questions:

1. Does God command His people to make sacrifices and burnt offerings?
2. What does God mean when He says, "I desire steadfast love and not sacrifice" if He wants sacrifices?
3. What is a covenant, and what does this have to do with Hosea 6:6? (See v. 7.)

The Old Testament is full of required sacrifices and burnt offerings (for example, Exodus 20:24; 23:18; Leviticus 1, 3, 4, 7, and 8). God obviously wanted sacrifices and burnt offerings, so why would He say otherwise? Interpreting a passage like Hosea 6:6 in harmony with the rest of Scripture leads us to understand that Hosea means "I desire steadfast love far more than sacrifice, the knowledge of God far more than burnt offerings." This is confirmed by David in Psalm 51. There (in vv. 16–17), he writes:

> For You will not delight in sacrifice, or I would give it;
> You will not be pleased with a burnt offering.
> The sacrifices of God are a broken spirit;
> a broken and contrite heart, O God, You will not despise.

A right relationship with God, based on saving faith in Him and whole-hearted commitment to Him, forms the basis for acceptable offerings and sacrifices. Without the faith-based relationship, the offerings and sacrifices accomplish nothing. When the relationship is right, when the people trust in Him and put their faith into action, David adds, "Then You will delight in right sacrifices, in burnt offerings and whole burnt offerings; then bulls will be offered on Your altar" (Psalm 51:19).

The covenant God establishes with His people is built upon His grace, received through faith. Faith in God shows itself in faithfulness to the covenant, external obedience flowing from internal faith. Adam lost faith and broke the covenant God had made with him (Hosea 6:7). Israel likewise broke faith, so it made little difference whether they offered sacrifices or not. At the heart of their relationship with God, Israel needed to remember their sin and God's grace. God demonstrated this in the exodus, where He revealed Himself as their only Savior (Hosea 13:4).

When Jesus cites Hosea 6:6, He makes the same point. In Matthew 9:11, the Pharisees criticized Him for eating with tax collectors and sinners. Jesus responds by pointing out the need that these sinners have for a Savior (9:12). He then directs them to Hosea 6:6a. If the Pharisees understood Scripture, they would realize that they, too, are sinners in need of a Savior. Moreover, God delights in showing mercy and compassion. He will punish sin, but He finds joy in forgiving repentant sinners.

When the Lord explained the First Commandment (Exodus 20:3–6), He said that He would punish people to the third and fourth generations of those who hate Him, but that He would show His love to a thousand generations of those who love Him and keep His commandments (faith in God and faithful living according to His covenant). We might put this in mathematical terms: God prefers mercy to punishment by a ratio of 250 or 333 to 1. Obviously, we can't say it quite like that, but we can understand that the big picture of Scripture is our sin and God's grace, brought together in the person of Jesus Christ, crucified and risen for us.

Jesus again quotes Hosea 6:6 in Matthew 12:7. Here, the disciples of Jesus are picking heads of grain, rubbing them together, and blowing away the chaff. This took place on the Sabbath, and the Pharisees considered these actions to be harvesting and threshing. Since harvesting and threshing are work, and since work was forbidden on the Sabbath, the Pharisees accuse Jesus' disciples of breaking God's Law. Jesus responds by referring to the time when David and his companions ate the consecrated bread at the tabernacle (Matthew 12:4), and mentions the fact that the priests work on the Sabbath and no one accuses them of wrongdoing (Matthew 12:5). He then adds Hosea 6:6, which speaks to the attitude of the Pharisees and their (lack of a) faith-relationship with God.

From the context, it appears that Jesus considers His disciples innocent of wrongdoing in this matter. They did not set out to harvest with sickles, nor did they form a threshing crew. They simply took what they needed at the moment, as did David with the consecrated bread, and ate. Jesus, the Lord of the Sabbath, declares them innocent. What attitude would a person have to have to condemn these innocent men for feeding themselves? Based on Hosea 6:6, the Pharisees reveal an attitude of unbelief and covenant unfaithfulness.

As we interpreted Scripture in harmony with itself, we followed these steps:

1. Checked the original context of Hosea 6:6.
2. Confirmed our understanding of Hosea 6:6 with Psalm 51.
3. Applied our interpretation of Hosea 6:6 to the use that Jesus made of it in Matthew 9:13 and 12:7, being careful to look at the contexts of each of these passages. In other words, we relied upon the oneness of Holy Scripture.

The Way of Eternal Life

Do we inherit eternal life based on our fulfillment of the Mosaic Law or as a gift by grace through faith in Jesus Christ?

A lawyer (an expert in the Hebrew Scriptures and the traditions that applied the Mosaic Law to everyday life) asked Jesus that very question: "Teacher, what shall I do to inherit eternal life?" (Luke 10:25). Surprisingly, Jesus responds with a question: "What is written in the Law? How do you read it?" (v. 26). The man quotes Deuteronomy 6:5 (love God) and Leviticus 19:18 (love your neighbor). Jesus responds approvingly: "You have answered correctly; do this, and you will live" (Luke 10:28). It might appear at this point that Jesus teaches the way of eternal life is obedience to the Mosaic Law, contradicting the rest of Scripture (see John 14:1–6; Romans 3:19–31; Ephesians 2:8–9) and rendering the cross unnecessary.

Sensitivity to the literary and cultural context along with an awareness of the clear teaching of Scripture helps the reader avoid a grave misunderstanding. The lawyer seeks to justify himself (Luke 10:29)—that is, provide a basis for claiming fulfillment of the Mosaic Law before God on Judgment Day. In order to do this, he must narrow the definition of "neighbor" to a manageable group. Jesus tells the parable of the Good Samaritan to help the lawyer see that there are no limits to "neighbor"—our neighbor is ultimately everyone in the world. Using the figure of a Samaritan (deep animosity and hatred existed between the Jews and the Samaritans at that time), Jesus drives home the point that no one can fulfill the Mosaic Law. His command "You go, and do likewise" (v. 37) leaves the lawyer in a hopeless position. This is the effect of God's holy Law on sinners—it kills us and leaves us in despair.

The reader of Luke's Gospel does not stop with verse 37, however. In Luke 10:38–42, we find the way of eternal life revealed clearly. Mary, doing nothing at all, inherits eternal life as she sits at the feet of Jesus. She has the "one thing" that is necessary for eternal life: faith in Jesus. This cannot be taken from her, no matter what happens (Luke 10:42). This is the effect of God's wonderful Gospel—it makes us alive and fills us with joy.

By remembering the rule of faith (the teaching of Scripture as a whole) and the clear passages that speak to this subject (illuminating the harder-to-understand texts), we leave Luke 10:25–42 with a renewed appreciation for Jesus and the gift of salvation that He has won for us by His obedience to the Law and His sacrifice for us under that same Law. (In chapter 6, we will explore the likewise helpful distinction between Law and Gospel, sin and grace.)

The Divinity of Christ

Does Jesus claim to be God or not?

He is clearly a human being—born of Mary (Matthew 1:18–25), raised in Nazareth (Luke 2:39–40), a carpenter by trade (Mark 6:3). But does He claim to be true God as well?

Some passages seem to suggest that He does not claim to be true God. In John 14:28, Jesus states that "the Father is greater than I." In Mark 13:32, He seems to say that He does not know when Judgment Day will take place: "But concerning that day or that hour, no one knows, not even the angels in heaven, nor the Son, but only the Father."

Other texts clearly reveal His claim to be true God. In John 8:58, Jesus proclaims: "Truly, truly, I say to you, before Abraham was, I am." The phrase "I am" translates two Greek words in the original that are identical to the name of God in the Greek translation of Exodus 3:14, where the Lord reveals His name to Moses before the exodus. Considering the fact that Abraham lived about two thousand years before the earthly ministry of Jesus, it is abundantly clear that Jesus claims to be true God in John 8:58 (emphasized by the oath formula "truly, truly"). Jesus also confesses, "I and the Father are one" (John 10:30).

How do these pieces fit together to make a coherent picture?

We might begin by remembering that Jesus did not always and fully use His divine power during His earthly ministry (from His conception to His death on the cross). We sometimes call this His "state of humiliation." He did not empty Himself of His divinity nor did He set aside His divine nature in any way, but He did not always use it, "humbling" Himself in obedience to the Father (see Philippians 2:6–11). The rule of faith reminds us that, although Jesus is fully human, He always was and always is fully and completely God.

The rule of faith also reflects the truth that God is triune. That is, God is one (Deuteronomy 6:4) and three (Matthew 28:18–20). Although the word *Trinity* doesn't appear in the Bible, the numbers and thoughts that make up the word certainly do ("Tri" means three; "-une" means one). Christians have long used this word to express this three-in-one divine complexity. Three persons, one being—each person fully and completely God yet together only one. We see Scripture distinguish the persons of the Godhead by their internal relationship with each other. The Father begets the Son from eternity. The Son is begotten of the Father from eternity (see John 1:1–18). The Spirit proceeds eternally from the Father and the Son (see John 14:26).

Within the Godhead, the Father is the head and the Son is the glory (1 Corinthians 11:3, somewhat analogous to the relation of man and woman in marriage). Even when Jesus always and fully uses His divine power, He submits Himself to the Father (1 Corinthians 15:24–28). The New Testament always carefully safeguards this relationship of Father, Son, and Holy Spirit. For example, where Jesus declares, "I and the Father are one," the original word for "one" is neuter (a thing) rather than masculine (a person). Jesus does not claim to be the Father, but reveals His essential unity with the Father (and the Spirit)—one God. Statements made by Jesus that reflect His personal relationship with the Father (not entirely unlike that of an earthly son to his father) should not be misunderstood as a comment on His nature as true God.

The rule of faith serves as a useful tool for the reader of Holy Scripture, especially when the really complex doctrines appear in the text (such as the Trinity or the nature of Christ). We are blessed to have the three great creeds—the Apostles', the Nicene, and the Athanasian—as summaries of the faith Scripture teaches and we confess. We want to keep these confessions close at hand when reading Scripture, the way we keep a ruler close at hand on our desks, to avoid mistakes we can make when we see only part of the picture.

Chapter 4 Note

1. On the Creed §1.

Chapter 5

Interpret Scripture in View of Christ

You search the Scriptures because you think that in them you have eternal life; and it is they that bear witness about Me.

—Jesus Christ (John 5:39)

Defining the Principle

THIS PRINCIPLE COMES FROM THE CONVICTION THAT JESUS Christ is the focal point of the entire Scripture. If somebody asks, "What is the single point toward which all of the Bible directs the reader?" the answer would be "Jesus Christ." In this section, we will consider several passages that give us this answer and help us keep Christ in the center when we read Scripture.

Applying the Principle

Acts 8:26–40

Read Acts 8:26–40 and answer the following questions:

1. Who are the two main characters in this story?
2. What passage from the Old Testament was the eunuch reading?

3. How could Philip hear him?
4. Why does the eunuch want to be baptized?

The eighth chapter of Acts continues the story of how the Gospel (or Good News) of Jesus Christ spread from Jerusalem to Rome. Stephen, the first martyr, is stoned to death in Acts 7 for testifying to Jesus as the Christ, the Son of God. A persecution of Christians followed that incident. Because of the persecution, Christians were scattered throughout the Roman province of Judea-Samaria (fulfilling the promise of Jesus in Acts 1:8). The brief account of this persecution in Acts 8:1–3 contains a fair amount of irony: instead of crushing the Christian movement, persecution spread it to points outside of Jerusalem, just as Jesus had planned!

Luke continues his record with two more accounts. They form a tremendous contrast and also contain a strong element of irony. In the first incident (Acts 8:9–25), Simon the sorcerer tries to buy the power that he sees Peter and John using to throw demons out of possessed people. Since this power was a gift from the Holy Spirit, it could not be bought.

In the next account (Acts 8:26–40), Philip shares the Gospel with an Ethiopian eunuch, a court official of a country south of Egypt. He comes to faith, is baptized, and rejoices in his salvation. Contrast the Ethiopian eunuch with Simon the sorcerer, and you will see a picture of a man who tried to buy what he could not (Simon) next to a picture of a man who received freely what he could not buy (the eunuch). The sorcerer, at the end of his story, is pleading for Peter's intercession so that nothing bad happens to him for trying to buy the Holy Spirit. The eunuch, at the end of his story, goes on his way rejoicing. Both men believed, but one of them lost sight of what his faith was all about. He saw the powerful gifts of the Spirit and wanted them for his own selfish purposes. The other man saw Jesus clearly in a passage from Isaiah and experienced the joy of his salvation.

The story of the Ethiopian eunuch helps us realize the importance of a Christ-centered understanding of the Bible. As the eunuch was reading Isaiah 53:7–8, Philip overheard him (as he was directed to do). This was possible because ancient manuscripts were written in capital letters with no spacing or punctuation between words and sentences. Imagine trying to read a book like that! One had to read out loud, sounding out the words. Because of this, Philip could hear the eunuch.

The eunuch was reading part of the fourth Suffering Servant Song,[1] a prophecy about the coming Savior (Isaiah 52:13–53:12). Specifically, the eunuch was reading Isaiah's description of the trial and execution of the coming Messiah. In fulfillment of this passage, Jesus stood before Pilate, refused to answer the charges against Him, and was executed. (See Matthew 26:63; Mark 14:61; and John 19:9.) Through Philip's sermon, the eunuch comes to faith in Jesus as his Savior and Lord and, as a result, seeks Baptism.[2] Acts 6:5 introduces Philip as one of the seven so-called deacons who were chosen to administer a widows' welfare fund in Jerusalem. We meet Philip again in Acts 8:4–5, where he, because of the persecution in Jerusalem, has gone to a city in Samaria and there preached Christ. Because of the miraculous signs Philip performed, people paid close attention to what he said. He spoke the Gospel, and people believed in Jesus. As a result, "there was much joy in that city" (Acts 8:8).

Scriptures Point Directly to Jesus

Note the parallels between this incident and the story of the Ethiopian eunuch. Philip points the Samaritans to Christ and later shows to the eunuch this same Savior. Both are "disadvantaged" with regard to their covenant standing.[3] Both come to faith in Christ and, at the end of their story, experience great joy. At the center of it all, prophesied by Isaiah, is Jesus Christ crucified for the sins of the world and raised to life on the third day for our justification.[4]

Philip and Jesus use the same principle of biblical interpretation. When Philip reads Scripture, he sees Jesus. This is exactly what Jesus says in Luke 24:25–26 when He is on the road to Emmaus with two of His disciples on the day He rose from the dead. They do not recognize Jesus because God kept them from doing so (v. 16). When they express their sadness that Jesus was crucified, He says, "O foolish ones, and slow of heart to believe all that the prophets have spoken! Was it not necessary that the Christ should suffer these things and enter into His glory?" (vv. 25–26). Jesus reveals the Christ-centered principle when He says that the central point of what the prophets have written is the person, death, and resurrection of the Christ. Luke confirms this in Luke 24:27 when he adds, "And beginning with Moses and all the Prophets, He interpreted to them in all the Scriptures the things concerning Himself." The *entire* Scripture points us to Christ Jesus, our Savior and Lord.

Scriptures Point Indirectly to Jesus

In addition to pointing directly to Jesus, the Scriptures also point *indirectly* to Jesus. They show us patterns that later are repeated and fulfilled. For example, in the exodus, the angel of death passes over those houses that have the blood of the lamb on their doorposts (see Exodus 12). The lamb is to be a male lamb in his prime, and no bones may be broken. When Jesus goes to Jerusalem for the last time in His earthly ministry, He discusses with Elijah and Moses the exodus[5] He is about to accomplish there (Luke 9:31). When Jesus dies, a male in His prime, the soldiers do not follow the normal procedure of breaking the victim's legs. Thereby Scripture could be fulfilled: "Not one of His bones will be broken" (John 19:36, based on Exodus 12:46, also referenced in Numbers 9:12; David echoes this promise in Psalm 34:20 as well). Since the Gospel of John records an instance where John the Baptist called Jesus the "Lamb of God" (John 1:29, 36), we can see Christ clearly in the Passover, a pattern of salvation that is fulfilled at the cross and also the Lord's Supper.

Scriptures Foreshadow Jesus

We also see Christ as the center of Scripture when we note how various events in the Old Testament foreshadow Jesus and His mission. In John 3:14, Jesus reveals to a Pharisee named Nicodemus that He has come from heaven. He is to be "lifted up," a phrase that could be interpreted in a number of different ways. Jesus makes plain what He means: "And as Moses lifted up the serpent in the wilderness, so must the Son of Man be lifted up, that whoever believes in Him may have eternal life" (John 3:14–15). Jesus does not say that the bronze serpent represents Him or is in some way a pattern He will follow, but He states that He will be lifted up like Moses lifted up the bronze serpent. Two points of contact emerge: (1) "Lifting up" does not refer to Jesus' resurrection from the dead or His ascension into heaven. When Jesus uses the phrase "lifted up," He refers to His crucifixion. (2) People will be rescued by believing God's promise (John 3:15).

We find the account of the bronze serpent in Numbers 21:4–9. The people of God are in the Sinai wilderness during the forty years between the exodus and the conquest of Canaan. Moses determined to go around Edom rather than face that nation in war. The people grew impatient and grumbled against both God and Moses. As a result, God sent poisonous snakes among them and many people died. When the people repented, they also asked Moses to intercede for them, which he did. God told Moses to make a bronze snake and put it up on a pole. Whoever looked at it, including those bitten by a poisonous snake, lived. The bronze serpent became the means God used to elicit a faith response from His people. The bronze serpent did not have the power to heal, but God did. The people of Moses' day were rescued from death by trusting in God's promise and acting on it. The bronze serpent hanging on a pole served as the means by which God accomplished this rescue.

Like the bronze serpent, Jesus explains to Nicodemus, He will be "lifted up." Jesus uses this same language again in John 12:32, where He says that He "will draw all people to Myself," perhaps alluding to the fact that the Israelites were drawn to the bronze serpent for their rescue. And, just as in Numbers 21, people will be saved by trusting in God's promise. In this case, God's promise is Jesus, crucified for the sins of the world. The rescue that God accomplishes through the cross is not simply a rescue from physical death but a rescue from God's righteous judgment against sinners. Jesus offers eternal life to all who look to Him in faith (as He says in John 3:15).

The Central Focus of Scripture

John 20:30–31 also points to Jesus Christ as the central focus of Scripture. Here, John tells us the reason he wrote his Gospel. John mentions the fact that Jesus did many miracles that he did not record. John then adds, "But these are written so that you may believe that Jesus is the Christ, the Son of God, and that by believing you may have life in His name."

John's purpose in writing his Gospel is identical to the purpose of the Bible as a whole. The Bible is not primarily an instruction manual for good works, although it serves admirably to that end. It is not merely the human record of religious thought among certain peoples and cultures in the Near East, although real people from that area were inspired to write it. The most important thing the Holy Spirit does through Scripture is bring people to a personal faith in Jesus Christ as Savior and Lord. Paul links faith and works together in discussing the purpose of the Bible, but keeps faith in Jesus as the first (and primary) purpose. Writing to Timothy, Paul says, "From childhood you have been acquainted with the sacred writings, which are able to make you wise for salvation through faith in Christ Jesus. All Scripture is breathed out by God and profitable for teaching, for reproof, for correction, and for training in righteousness, that the man of God may be complete, equipped for every good work" (2 Timothy 3:15–17).

Each time we open our Bibles, we should ask how they point us to Jesus as our Savior and Lord. Failure to do so weakens or even removes the comfort and hope God provides in this sacred book.

Chapter 5 Notes

1. In four places, Isaiah prophesies a coming servant of the Lord who will suffer (that is, die) for the sins of the world: Isaiah 42; 49; 50; and 52–53. These poetic sections are called the Suffering Servant Songs. Parts of the fourth song (52:13–53:12) appear throughout the New Testament: Matthew 8:17; Luke 22:37; John 12:38; Romans 10:16; 15:21; 1 Peter 2:22, 24.
2. You may notice that some later Greek manuscripts add a few lines to Acts 8:36, making it clear to the reader that the eunuch believes in Jesus and seeks Baptism for that reason. How we got our Bible will be covered in chapter 16.
3. In both his Gospel and the Book of Acts, Luke shows a concern for outcasts and those on the bottom of the social ladder. Jews generally hated the Samaritans, and a eunuch (who could not have children) could not even fulfill the first command God gave ("Be fruitful and multiply," Genesis 1:28). Yet these are the people brought to Christ by the Holy Spirit in Acts 8!
4. *Justification* is a legal term that not only means "to be declared innocent," but also, in light of Ezekiel 18:5–9, declared by God to have fulfilled all our covenant obligations (such as the Ten Commandments). This "right status" is freely credited by faith in Jesus Christ, not because we are innocent or have done what the Law requires.
5. English versions differ in their translation of the Greek word *exodos.* The New King James Version offers "decease" (that is, departure from life), while the English Standard Version and the New International Version render it "departure." No doubt it does refer to Jesus' coming crucifixion, but the choice of the word *exodos* certainly also calls to mind Exodus 12, when the Israelites crossed the Red Sea.

Chapter 6

Distinguish Law and Gospel, Sin and Grace

The promise is distinct from the law; and since they are different, they cannot be mixed.

—Tyconius[1]

Defining the Principle

PERHAPS YOU HAVE LEARNED A SIMPLE FORMULA FOR DIStinguishing the Law and the Gospel promise: in the Law, God tells us what to do; in the Gospel, God tells us what He has done for us. (SOS: The Law Shows us Our Sins. The Gospel Shows us Our Savior.)

That formula sounds simple. Sometimes it *is* too simple, and sometimes it isn't. In this chapter, we shall examine four portions of Scripture: Genesis 2–3; Exodus 20:1–17; Ephesians 2:8–10; and Romans 6:1–14 in order to explore the art of distinguishing Law and Gospel, sin and grace.

Applying the Principle

Genesis 2–3

God created Adam and Eve without sin. In this sinless state, they did not need God's written Law to show them the difference between right and wrong. However, in Genesis 2:17 God reveals His first "shall not." He says, "Of the tree of the knowledge of good and evil you shall not eat." With these words, God provided a way for Adam and Eve to show their love to Him—by not eating from the tree of the knowledge of good and evil. Only a few verses later, in Genesis 3:6, we read that both Adam and Eve ate of the fruit. In so doing, they sinned. God had given them the command (Law) to avoid eating from that one tree, permitting them to eat from all the others in the garden. Intended as a guide for faithful obedience, the Law now became a mirror, showing them their transgression. They responded by trying to hide from God (3:8).

During the conversation that follows, God speaks a word of hope: "I will put enmity between you and the woman, and between your offspring and her offspring; He shall bruise your head, and you shall bruise His heel" (3:15). Adam and Eve receive the good news that the Lord will win the ultimate victory over Satan. Good news indeed for two people in a hopeless situation!

Law and Gospel, prominent already in the first three chapters of the Bible, continue to serve as filters through which we read all of Scripture. We look next at the Ten Commandments. We'll then move on to a few passages from Paul's letters where faith (Gospel) and works (Law) are distinguished and their proper relationship revealed. We find the Ten Commandments in Exodus 20 and Deuteronomy 5.

Exodus 20:1–17

Sometimes people think they have to do good works to be saved, or that they have to keep the Ten Commandments so that God will love them.[2] A quick check on the original context of the Commandments helps us understand that God did not give us these rules so that we could save ourselves or earn His love.

God gave the Commandments about one and a half months after He rescued the Hebrews from Egypt in the original exodus (see Exodus 19:1). Before Moses gives the people the Commandments (Law), he reminds them that God has saved them by grace (Gospel): "I am the Lord your God, who brought you out of the land of Egypt, out of the house of slavery" (Exodus 20:2; see also Deuteronomy 5:6).

In short, God did not give the Law to the Hebrews so they could save themselves. God had saved them a month and a half earlier. His love for them springs from within Him, not from their obedience to the Commandments. Before God gave the Ten Commandments, He had rescued them, carrying them on "eagles' wings" out of slavery and death to be with Him (Exodus 19:4).

The Purpose of the Law

If God did not give the Law so people could save themselves, why did He give it at all? God's Law served as a guide for His people. Now that God had rescued them from Egypt, what did He expect of them?

The New Testament often asks a similar question: now that we have been brought to faith in Jesus Christ, what are we to do with our lives? In the Old Testament as well as in the New Testament, putting our faith into practice is an important part of our calling.

In both testaments, God calls His people a "kingdom of priests" (or "royal priesthood") and a "holy nation" (see Exodus 19:6 and 1 Peter 2:9). Priests offer sacrifices, and a holy nation is a nation of people set apart for service to God. Unlike the sacrificial victims of Old Testament days, we Christians offer our whole lives as sacrifices (Romans 12:1). We give back to God our bodies and souls and everything we have in gratitude for what Christ has done for us on the cross.

Thus, the Ten Commandments served as a guide for God's people, and God's Law continues to serve Christians in this way. The Law also shows us our sins (as stated earlier in the chapter), and curbs evil impulses with the threat of punishment.[3] But the Law cannot save.

God's Law is bigger than the Ten Commandments. Throughout the Old Testament, God gives His people directives for how they are to live in society, how they are to offer sacrifices and other religious duties, and what type of morality they are to practice. Keeping God's Law entails more than avoiding sin. It involves not only avoiding the wrong but doing the right. It includes an obligation to take care of people who need our help. We see this in both the Old Testament (Ezekiel 18:5–9) and the New Testament (James 1:27). Martin Luther highlighted this obligation in his explanations of the Ten Commandments. After the negatives ("so that we do not") he stated the positives ("but that we do").

Ephesians 2:8–10

The proper distinction between Law and Gospel is of critical importance, because when we confuse the two we can lose the assurance of our salvation. If my salvation depends on me, even if it depends only a tiny, tiny bit on me, how can I be sure that I have done my "bit" just right?

To be absolutely sure of our salvation, we must recognize that it depends absolutely and only on Jesus Christ. The lives we lead after we are brought to faith in Jesus Christ are lived that way *because* we have been saved, not *in order* to be saved. Paul keeps the relationship between Law and Gospel in balance throughout his letters, and we can see it particularly in Ephesians 2:8–10 and Romans 6:1–11.

In Ephesians 2, Paul describes the contrast between the former life of his Christian readers and their present life. Before the Gospel came to them, they were condemned by God (as are all people by nature). Now, having come to faith in Jesus Christ, they are rescued from God's righteous anger against sinners on the Last Day. Paul describes this contrast twice: first in 2:1–10 and then in slightly different terms in 2:11–22. Read 2:4–10 and answer the following questions:

1. What moved God to save sinners?
2. What is the source of saving faith?
3. How do good works figure into the equation of salvation?

The Bible often mentions God's *grace*. Depending on the translation, Paul uses the term at least a dozen times in Ephesians alone.[4] We can define grace very simply as "undeserved love." God saves sinners through faith in Jesus Christ. This is the only way of salvation in all history and in all the world.

What moved God to send His one and only Son so that whoever believes in Him would not perish but have eternal life? God's love motivated Him, a love we do not deserve, but which He pours out on us richly in Jesus Christ (see Ephesians 2:7). By the gracious gift of God—Jesus Christ—people are saved. Note what Paul says, though; they are saved through faith. This faith is not a decision we make to believe in God, but a gift from God. Paul could hardly have said it more clearly. God gives us the faith we need to personally receive the benefits of Jesus' sacrifice on Calvary. It is important to keep this in mind, for faith is a Gospel gift, not a result of the Law.

We do make a contribution to our life with God, but that does not come at the point of conversion. God is the one who brings us into His family (Gospel); once we are members of His family, we seek to live out His will for our lives (Law). But our salvation depends entirely on what He has done and continues to do for us (Gospel).

In a sense, living the Christian life is easy. God has made us His own special people, and He has even prepared good works in advance for us to do. He provides us the opportunities and the resources to help feed the hungry, speak up for the oppressed, help our neighbor, and the like. Living our lives for Jesus should be the easiest thing in the world, right? But the fact is, putting our faith into practice is very hard—even impossible when we rely upon our own power instead of the power God provides through the Gospel.

Some have compared the Christian life to dieting. We succeed (at least to a degree) for a while, but over the long haul we often seem to lose the ground we gained. We cover the same territory in our lives over and over and over. But in Christ Jesus, we get up and try again, trusting Him for forgiveness and help. As we do so, we know that His love for us is secure (Gospel) and that in His strength we live out our faith according to His purpose for us on earth (Law). Even as we live, we await the time He calls us home (Gospel).

Romans 6:1–14

Written three or four years earlier than Ephesians, Paul traces the same relationship between Law and Gospel in Romans 6:1–14. He anchors our sanctification (Christian lifestyle) in our justification (God's declaration that we are sinless and have fulfilled His covenant demands), specifically, in our Baptism. God's gift of salvation to us (Gospel) becomes our motivation for holy living (keeping the Law). Based on Romans 6:1–14, answer the following:

1. What happens to a person in the process of being baptized?
2. What does the resurrection of Jesus Christ from the dead mean to us?
3. What kind of relationship does the Christian have with sin?

We can compare being baptized to taking a trip. We are first carried back to the death of Jesus where we are buried with Him and washed clean of our sins in His blood. We are then transported to the future, to Judgment Day, where we see God keep His promise to us in our Baptism, that "Whoever believes and is baptized will be saved" (Mark 16:16). We finally return to our own time, the present day, where we live each day in a new way. We live for the glory of God and not our own welfare. We live as servants of the Lord Jesus, not as slaves to sin. We live free from the demands of the Law, filled with the Gospel, free to show Christ's love in all that we say and do.

Very soon, we realize that we still struggle with sin. In Romans 7 (especially vv. 14–25), Paul expresses the frustration every Christian has in trying to live the way Jesus has called us to live. But even our failure to live according to God's will (Law) does not rob us of the great comfort of knowing that our salvation is secure in Jesus Christ (Gospel). We rejoice in this, not that it should become a license for sin, but that we have a freedom from fear and are called to serve Him who gave everything for us. Keeping Law and Gospel distinct makes it possible to live in the joy of our salvation in spite of our success or failure in applying our faith to our daily lives.

Chapter 6 Notes

1. Book of Rules, Part III.
2. There seem to be eleven commandments in both Exodus and Deuteronomy, but since they are called the Ten Commandments (Exodus 34:28; Deuteronomy 4:13; 10:4), we number ten. Roman Catholics, Lutherans, and some other Protestants number Exodus 20:3–5a as the First Commandment, and divide verse 17 to become the Ninth and Tenth Commandments. Many other Protestants list verses 4–5a as the Second Commandment, and keep all of verse 17 as the Tenth Commandment. God, however, does not number the commandments.
3. Protestants traditionally number these uses of the Law as follows: the Law curbs evil impulses with the threat of punishment (first use); shows us our sins (second use); and serves as a guide for God's people (third use). These distinctions are rooted in the observations of the Early and Medieval Church Fathers.
4. The same Greek or Hebrew word can often be translated with a variety of English words. When doing a word study in the Bible, it can be helpful to check several different translations.

Chapter 7

The "Then and There" Meaning and the "Here and Now" Meaning

As in a meadow, I perceive in what has been read a great diversity of flowers. . . . The reading of the divine Scriptures is not a meadow only, but a paradise; for the flowers here have not a mere fragrance only, but fruit too, capable of nourishing the soul.

—John Chrysostom[1]

AS WE KNOW FROM EVERYDAY LIFE, COMMUNICATION CAN be hard work, both for the writer and the reader (or speaker and listener). It is easy to misunderstand what someone else writes or says. Bible students, too, often misinterpret passages. Let's use an absurd example to illustrate this.

Once upon a time in a Bible study far, far away, two men were arguing about what kind of vehicle Jesus used when He rode into Jerusalem (Matthew 21). The first man argued that Jesus drove a Dodge product, because verse 7 says He rode in on a Colt, and Dodge makes a car called a Colt. Then the second man argued that Jesus drove a Ford because Colt has four letters and so does the word *Ford*. He argued that *colt* was a special code word that really meant Ford. Which of the two was right?

The first man made the mistake of thinking that Jesus lived in twenty-first century America. As silly as this sounds, many people make mistakes very similar to this because they fail to realize that Jesus spoke as a first-century Galilean Jew to people of that region and time. The second man made the mistake of thinking that the Bible is full of secret codes, where numbers and animals and events hide secret meanings that only a few "insiders" know about. Again, this sounds very silly, but it is an approach that some take to Bible study. We will see a symbolic use of numbers in apocalyptic writing,[2] but no such secret codes exist.

In *Learning to Use Your Bible* (Concordia, 1969), Oscar Feucht offers three basic questions to ask when studying the Bible:

1. What does the passage say?
2. What does the passage mean?
3. What does the passage mean for us—for me?

What Does the Passage Say?

The first of these questions asks us to read the text carefully. Do we know what all the individual words mean? After all, words can sometimes mean many different things, depending on usage and context. Take the word *cat* as an example. When you use this word, you probably refer to a domestic house cat—small, furry, and friendly. But *cat* can also refer to the large predators of Africa and Asia such as lions, tigers, and leopards. We can also use the word *cat* figuratively, as it was used in pop culture, to refer to someone of a particular attitude and dress (e.g., a "cool cat" in the 1960s).

Words can also have technical meanings in addition to their everyday meanings. We can use the word *prayer* to illustrate this point. Normally, *prayer* refers to our communication with God. But in some states, in legal contexts, *prayer* refers to the amount the plaintiff is seeking from the defendant in a lawsuit.

A particular writer may also use a word or a group of words with one specific meaning in mind. For example, look at the verb *save*. This word means "to rescue" and can be used to describe various kinds of rescues. If a man is rescued from a ship or a woman is rescued from a fire, we can use the word *save* to refer to that rescue. But what about those times when Jesus says, "Your faith has saved you"[3] (Luke 7:50)? Does He mean someone has been healed because they believed in Him (saved from disease or disability), or does He mean they have been rescued from the Law's condemnation on Judgment Day? In Luke's Gospel, a particular phrase appears four times: "your faith has saved you/made you well." It has the same word order, vocabulary, and verb tense in the original Greek in all four places. What does Luke mean when He quotes Jesus? The first time Jesus says "your faith has saved you," He says it to a sinful woman who washes His feet with her tears and dries them with her hair (Luke 7:36–50). Since no physical healing has occurred, and since Jesus states plainly "your sins are forgiven" (v. 48), the translator knows that "save" refers to "saved from condemnation" and correctly translates "Your faith has saved you; go in peace" (v. 50).

In Luke 8:48, Jesus says, "Your faith has saved you" to a woman who was healed when she touched His robe. He says the same thing to a leper who has been healed in Luke 17:19 and to a blind beggar he has healed in 18:42. Most translators render "your faith has saved you" as "your faith has healed you" or "your faith has made you well" (as in the ESV). However, the use of this identical phrase in Luke 7:50, clearly referring to salvation from eternal condemnation, suggests that more than salvation from disease or disability is intended.

We see this confirmed in Luke 17:19. Jesus says "your faith has saved you" only to the Samaritan leper. All ten lepers were made well, but only the Samaritan leper returns to Jesus, falls at His feet, and gives Him thanks. He alone hears the words "your faith has saved you."

The people in these four passages had a faith in Jesus, which saved them from God's judgment against sinners. Translators face the challenge of understanding how a particular author uses a word and the challenge of conveying that in their translation. This sensitivity to an author's pattern of usage of a word or phrase is really just an application of the principle that we use the clear passage to help us understand and translate the unclear or ambiguous passage.

The question "Do we know what all the words mean?" may look easy on the surface. At times, however, further study (such as applying the principles from part one) will provide deeper insights. To avoid the mistake of the man who thought *colt* referred to an automobile made by Dodge, we need to learn that words can have a variety of meanings. To tell what an author means by a particular word, we must trace his use of it throughout his writings.

Do we know what the text says? At times, Bible students overlook this basic step. Some say, for example, that Saul changed his name to Paul when he was converted. They may even claim that this change to Paul (a Latin word meaning "little") indicated his newly found humility. However, the Book of Acts contains no record of such a name change. Jesus confronts Saul and converts him in Acts 9. Luke (the author of Acts) does not call him Paul until Acts 13:9, on the first missionary journey, some twelve years after his conversion. Very likely, Saul had the name Paul from birth, one of three Latin names a Roman citizen would normally have. In any event, no textual evidence indicates that he acquired it at his conversion. Let's not skip the first step of Oscar Feucht's Bible study advice! If we do, we can easily miss material in the text or imagine things that never really took place.[4]

What Does the Passage Mean?

The second step is interpretation: what does this passage mean "then and there"? The answer to this question may involve some research into the historical or cultural background of the passage being studied. We can look at Matthew 1:18–19 for an example. Read these two verses and answer the following questions:

1. What is the relationship between Mary and Joseph at this time?
2. Why is Joseph called Mary's husband?
3. What does it mean when Matthew writes "before they came together"?
4. What qualities of Joseph do the words *just man* emphasize?
5. If they are only engaged, why does Joseph have to divorce her?

Matthew begins the section by noting that Mary was engaged (betrothed, pledged to be married) to Joseph when she became pregnant. In our culture, engagement is a verbal pledge usually accompanied by the giving of a ring. A second ring is given at the wedding ceremony. The practice in first-century Israel was quite different. A written contract bound engaged couples. Thus, the betrothal period (a minimum of nine months and a maximum of one year) was very formal and was legally binding. This also explains two other details in the story. Since they were bound by this engagement contract, they could be called husband and wife, though they could not live together. If they chose to nullify the engagement contract, they could do so. Since we don't have a binding contract for engagement, we don't have a word for dissolving an engagement contract, so translators use the term that refers to dissolution of a marriage contract. We call this divorce.

This text illustrates a problem that comes up from time to time in Bible study. Matthew knows first-century Jewish laws and customs. So do his original readers. Matthew wrote in Greek, which his original audience read. We live two thousand years removed from that time and half a world away from it. And as for Greek, very few of us know it well enough to be able to read it and understand it. This means that we must do homework when reading various parts of the Bible. This second step of Oscar Feucht's advice can challenge us.

Matthew makes it clear that Joseph did not father the baby Mary is now carrying. He writes "before they came together," an expression that refers to sexual intercourse. At the end of verse 20, we may describe the situation like this: Someone other than the man to whom she is engaged has caused Mary to become pregnant. Bound by an engagement contract, the same laws that applied to married people apply to her. The Old Testament penalty for adultery[5] is death, and so Mary should be put to death according to the Law (see Leviticus 20:10; Deuteronomy 22:22). However, the Romans rule Israel at this time. They do not permit a local people to try capital cases, reserving the "right of the sword" for themselves.[6] In Roman law, adultery was not a capital crime. Therefore the Jews cannot kill an adulteress. The rabbis decided that if they could not execute a woman for this crime, she must be regarded the same as dead. So they required that the husband divorce his adulterous wife.

Now, Joseph is a just man (one who keeps the Law; see Ezekiel 18:5–9). As a just man, he will divorce Mary—that is, void their engagement contract. Joseph's plan for the divorce reveals his character. Instead of making a public display of Mary, making sure that no one in their small village of Nazareth would blame him for the pregnancy, he plans to divorce her quietly, without a lot of fanfare. In short, he risks public embarrassment in order to minimize the shame that (he thinks) Mary will have to endure.

What have we learned about discovering the "then and there" meaning of this text? Joseph and Mary are engaged, a legally binding relationship. Mary becomes pregnant (through the miraculous activity of the Holy Spirit). Thus in the eyes of the Law, she becomes an adulteress. In reality, she is a virgin, but Joseph doesn't know this yet. Joseph is a law-abiding man and will do what he is required to do, but he reveals a noble character by deciding to divorce (nullify the engagement contract) Mary quietly.

As we can see, it sometimes takes work to put ourselves in the shoes (or sandals) of the original readers of the Bible. The various Bible study tools help us do this, but Bible study is really a lifelong adventure. There's always something "just around the corner" that may help us understand a passage with which we have previously struggled.

As we look for the meaning of the text, we often look for Bible teachers who can help us. As we do so, we need to remember that not everyone who stands up and says, "This is what the Greek (or Hebrew) means" is right. Human beings are often wrong.

However, someone who has spent his or her life in the Word can very often help others understand the Bible better. Note what happened to Apollos when he arrived in Ephesus. He was a learned man with a thorough knowledge of the Scriptures and taught about Jesus accurately. He was a great Bible teacher and evangelist, but he didn't know about Christian Baptism. So Priscilla and Aquila, a wife and husband team, instructed him more fully about the Christian faith (see Acts 18:24–26). No matter how much we know, there's always room to grow in the faith!

What Does the Passage Mean for Us—for Me?

We now turn to Oscar Feucht's third question: What does the passage mean for us—for me? (Answering this question includes applying the passage to your life: what does God teach me in this passage, and how will that affect what I believe and do?) People might answer this question in two ways:

- It means whatever I want it to mean.
- Stay as close to the original meaning as possible.

To illustrate these ways of answering the question, look again at Matthew 1:18–19. Some who interpret the text to mean whatever they want it to mean have concluded that God condones sexual activity before marriage but after engagement. They base this on the use of *husband* for Joseph, Mary's fiancé. If a husband may be intimate with his wife, and Joseph (who is only engaged) is called a *husband*, then God must approve intercourse between engaged couples. So the logic goes—logic based on a faulty answer to the question of what the passage means to our lives today.

To apply a passage to our lives accurately, we must stay as close to the original meaning as possible. Looking at Matthew 1:18–19, we discover that God gave us this text to teach us about Mary's virgin conception of Jesus by the Holy Spirit. Matthew also explained why Joseph did not divorce Mary in spite of the fact that he was a just (law-abiding) man. As was the custom of the day, Mary and Joseph did not engage in sexual activity prior to their wedding.

In these two verses, we see God at work, fulfilling His promise to send a Savior, born of a virgin (Matthew 1:23). God accomplishes salvation without any human help, even at the initial stage. We may learn from these verses that God is at work in the world and in our lives to accomplish His will, our salvation (as Paul says in 1 Timothy 2:4). God is at work in Mary's life, in Joseph's life, and in our lives to bring people to faith through the Gospel of Jesus Christ. This is true even when the events of our lives create problems (premarital pregnancy in the case of Mary) or challenge our Christian character (a pregnant fiancée for Joseph). God works all these things for the good—that is, for the salvation of His people (Romans 8:28–30). Under trying circumstances, they kept God's Word and showed compassion for one another. Their lives illustrate to us what God elsewhere calls us to believe and do.

Rahab's Lie, Joshua 2:1–7

A second example illustrates how readers may go astray when interpreting and applying a story. In Joshua 2:4–5, Rahab, a resident of Jericho, lies to her Canaanite countrymen to protect two Israelite spies. Some interpreters conclude from this story that it is okay to tell lies for a good cause, such as protecting someone.

Although it is true that God's people do not owe the truth to people who will use it for evil purposes, that does not mean God encourages us to lie. The Bible clearly and persistently teaches against lying (e.g., Exodus 20:16; Zechariah 8:16–17; Revelation 21:8). When Jesus faced questioning from opponents, He commonly answered evasively, answered with a question, or even remained silent (Matthew 21:23–27; 26:59–64; Mark 14:60–62; Luke 20:19–26; 22:67–70; 23:3). But He did not lie, leaving us a clear, though challenging, example to follow.

So then what should one conclude about the "here and now" meaning of Joshua 2:1–7? Based on the context of the chapter, one might conclude that Rahab is for us an example of a new believer who is still learning right from wrong and who is struggling to know what is best to do in a challenging situation. What is more, we may see that God still had mercy on her and her family, despite her weaknesses (Joshua 6:22–25).

Summary

When we read a passage in Scripture, we want to remember to ask and answer the first two questions before we apply a section of the Bible to our own lives:

1. What does the passage say?
2. What does the passage mean?
3. What does the passage mean for us—for me?

Chapter 7 Notes

1. *Concerning the Statues*, Homily I, 2.
2. "Apocalyptic" refers to a type of prophecy and to a literary genre where various kinds of symbolism are used.
3. Some translations use the English phrase "made you well" or "healed you" instead of "saved you."
4. Sometimes pictures in our minds prevent us from reading the text carefully. For example, the shape of the ark in Genesis 6 resembles a giant shoe box, not a ship. Yet, when the ark is mentioned, people usually think of some kind of boat. Or picture Elijah being taken to heaven. He did not travel in a fiery chariot. The text says he was taken into heaven by a whirlwind (2 Kings 2:1, 11). A fiery chariot separated Elijah and Elisha, but the whirlwind took Elijah up.
5. Adultery is a very specific crime in the Bible. God directs a man to avoid sexual contact with the wife of another man (Exodus 20:14; see also Jeremiah 29:23 and Romans 7:3; the commandment is written in a masculine singular form, though it would also properly apply to a woman who has sex with someone other than her husband). A man does not commit adultery just against the married woman with whom he has sexual contact but also against her husband. In our culture, *adultery* may denote sexual activity outside of marriage by either spouse, but the Hebrew word for *adultery* refers exclusively to a married or engaged person who has sexual contact with someone other

than his or her spouse or fiancé (as Brown-Driver-Briggs notes under the entry for *na'aph*). A man who has sexual relations with an unmarried woman, whether he is married, engaged, or single, must marry the girl or at least pay the "bride-price" (Exodus 22:16–17).

6. This same problem occurs in John 18:31, where the Jewish leaders must take Jesus to Pilate for execution rather than do it themselves.

Part Two
Interpreting Different Kinds of Scripture

Thus far, we have read primarily stories (prose or narrative accounts) in Scripture. These are perhaps the easiest biblical texts to begin with. In chapters 8, 9, 10, and 11, we will explore guidelines to follow four special kinds of biblical writing: poetry, prophecy, parables, and apocalyptic writing. Chapter 12 provides a summary of tools available to help you study Scripture.

Chapter 8

Poetry in the Bible

POETRY, LIKE PROSE, COMES IN A VARIETY OF STYLES. IN THE ancient world, poetry was used to tell stories. Examples from Greek literature include *The Iliad* and *The Odyssey* by Homer, written in the eighth century BC or earlier. This kind of poetry is called *narrative poetry* because it tells a story that has a beginning, a middle, and an end. Probably written long before Homer's works, the Book of Job serves as a good example of narrative poetry in the Bible.

By the fifth century BC, poets were using poetry to write plays. Works by Euripides, Sophocles, and Aristophanes fall into this category in the ancient world. Shakespeare is a more modern example of the same type of poetry. The Bible does not contain any of this kind of poetry.

A third type of poetry in Bible times is lyric poetry, poems intended to be read as the lyre (a stringed musical instrument) is played.[1] The Bible has a large number of this type of poem, most notably the Book of Psalms. Some also occur in the New Testament, for example, in Luke 1 and 2. The poetry we find in the Bible has some elements in common with poetry outside of the Bible, but it also differs in many ways. The poems in the Bible aren't based on a meter that we would ordinarily recognize, and biblical poetry does not usually rhyme.

Parallelism

The most obvious distinctive feature of Hebrew poetry is *parallelism*, a repetition of the thought in the first line expressed with some variation in the second line. The second line may say the same thing (synonymous) as the first line, may introduce an opposite thought, or may enrich (add emphasis to) the first line. This parallelism makes the poem (or psalm) especially useful in worship services, because it lends itself so readily to antiphonal reading or chanting. One part of the assembly says the first line, and the second part of the worshiping group repeats the thought of the first line but says it in a different way.

See Psalm 121 for each example of parallelism. The Hebrews used this psalm as a pilgrimage song, sung by people on the way to Jerusalem where the temple, the "embassy" of God on earth, was located. As pilgrims traveled up to Jerusalem, which is set on the top of a mountain, they could sing or chant this psalm in preparation for worship and sacrifice. This wonderful Gospel poem assures the believer of God's providence and care. As you read the psalm, notice how the poet has made his song sound natural, almost like a conversation or dialogue. Each of the second lines repeats or expands the thought in each of the first lines without sounding artificial or forced.

Historical Setting

When reading Hebrew poetry, especially the Psalms, it is very helpful to know the historical setting in which the poem was written. Psalm 51 provides a very good example of this. The heading of the psalm reads: "To the choirmaster. A Psalm of David, when Nathan the prophet went to him, after he had gone in to Bathsheba." If you don't know the story of David, Bathsheba, Uriah, and the prophet Nathan, it is a good idea to turn to 2 Samuel 11:1–12:25. David commits a variety of sins (including adultery and murder) but tries to cover them up. Only after being confronted by Nathan does David confess his sin and seek forgiveness. Out of that terrible tragedy comes this psalm, a heartfelt confession of sin and a joyful celebration of God's forgiveness.

As you read through Psalm 51, you may recognize several parts of it. Verses 10–11 appear as "Create in Me," or the Offertory, in many liturgical worship services. Several services use Psalm 51:15 ("O Lord, open my lips, and my mouth will declare Your praise") as a verse and response.

Some confessional services include verse 17 ("The sacrifices of God are a broken spirit; a broken and contrite heart, O God, You will not despise").

Worship and Biblical Poetry

Liturgical worship services draw heavily from the poetic sections of the Bible. The Venite ("O come, let us sing to the Lord") is Psalm 95:1–7 set to music. The Nunc Dimittis ("Lord, now You let Your servant go in peace") is the joyful song of Simeon in Luke 2:29–32. He took the infant Jesus in his arms and praised God, who had kept His promise that Simeon would see the Savior before His death. The Benedictus ("Blessed be the Lord God of Israel") comes from Zechariah, who sang that song when he was filled with the Holy Spirit following the naming of his son, John the Baptist (Luke 1:68–79). The Magnificat ("My soul magnifies the Lord") is Mary's song of joy over bearing the Christ Child (Luke 1:46–55). You might enrich your worship experience by investigating the origin of the elements in the worship services you use at your church.

Poetic Meanings

One word of caution is in order when interpreting biblical poetry. Figurative meanings, metaphors, and symbolic language are found somewhat more frequently in poetry than in prose. For example, David writes in Psalm 7:14–15, "Behold, the wicked man conceives evil and is pregnant with mischief and gives birth to lies. He makes a pit, digging it out, and falls into the hole that he has made." Men don't literally get pregnant, but the psalmist can use the metaphor of conception, pregnancy, and birth to make his point more vividly. He shifts to a second picture in verse 15, that of a man digging a hole. He makes his point clear in verse 16, "His mischief returns upon his own head, and on his own skull his violence descends." Or, as we might say, "You reap what you sow."

Background for the Psalms

You will also want to be aware that many psalms reflect earlier Scripture or celebrate the great saving acts of God in the past. If possible, read these background passages before interpreting the psalm you are studying. Genesis 1:26–28 forms the background to Psalm 8. Based on these two sections of Scripture, answer the following questions:

1. How would you describe the status of humanity in relation to the animals?
2. How would you describe the status of humanity in relation to God?
3. Why has God elevated humanity to such a high status?
4. How does the theory of evolution view humanity?

David, the author of Psalm 8, begins by contrasting the glory and magnificence of God with the relative unimportance of man. He uses parallelism to make his point in verse 4:

> What is man that You are mindful of him, and the son of man that You care for him?

David said the same thing twice, in different ways, to make the point more forceful. He then contrasts our apparent insignificance with the status God has granted us as His image and likeness (see Genesis 1:26–28), writing in verse 5:

> Yet You have made him a little lower than the heavenly beings[2] and crowned him with glory and honor.

God created humans in His image and likeness and appointed them as His representatives to rule over the earth. The theory of evolution tells us that we are essentially the same as the animals, particularly the primates. We may be at the top of the food chain now, but only by accident have we achieved this. Genesis 1–2 (and Psalm 8) reveals to us that we were created to be the "crown of creation," God's appointed managers of the earth, second only to Him in relation to the rest of creation. Yet the gulf between us and God is very great, as the psalmist confesses. However, God often chooses the lowly things of this world to reflect His mercy and praise (Psalm 8:2).

Messianic Psalms

Another feature of the psalms is that they are sometimes messianic. That is, they combine prophecy and poetry to portray the coming Savior. Psalm 2[3] (part two of a two-part introduction to the whole Book of Psalms) and Psalm 110[4] both serve as examples of messianic psalms, but none is more powerful than Psalm 22. Read Psalm 22 and identify details that pertain to Christ's crucifixion, recorded in Matthew 27:45–56; Mark 15:33–41; Luke 23:44–49; and John 19:16b–30. Keep in mind that this was written by David about one thousand years before Jesus died on the cross for the sins of the world.

Psalm 22:1

____

Psalm 22:6

____

Psalm 22:7

____

Psalm 22:8

____

Psalm 22:15

____

Psalm 22:16

____

Psalm 22:17

____

Enjoy the poetry of the Bible! As the Old Testament often celebrated God's deliverance of His people in psalms (Exodus 15; Psalms 74, 77–78, 105–106), so in the New Testament several poems or hymns rejoice in the Lord Jesus Christ (two of them are Philippians 2:5–11 and Colossians 1:15–20).

Chapter 8 Notes

1. Hebrew lyric poems date back to David, about 1000 BC. Classic Greek lyric poetry dates back to Pindar, about 500 BC.
2. The Hebrew word here is *Elohim*, a word that usually refers to God. Many translators think it refers to the angels, but it makes

good sense to understand it as a reference to God. By God's grace, humans were made to be His representatives on earth ("image and likeness"), second only to God in status.

3. Psalm 2:1 is quoted in Acts 4:25. Psalm 2:7 appears in Acts 13:33; Hebrews 1:5; and 5:5. And Psalm 2:9 is cited in Revelation 2:27; 19:15.
4. Jesus quotes Psalm 110:1 in Matthew 22:44; Mark 12:36; and Luke 20:42. It is also quoted in Acts 2:34; 1 Corinthians 15:25; and Hebrews 1:13. In the New Testament, it is the most often quoted Old Testament passage. Psalm 110:4 appears in Hebrews 5:6; 7:17, 21.

Chapter 9

Prophecy in the Bible

Old Testament

OLD TESTAMENT PROPHETS SPOKE FOR GOD. THEY ADMONished God's people, convicting them of their sins (Law). The prophets also spoke of God's mercy and compassion, encouraging the people to repent and believe (Gospel). Sometimes, during the course of their work, prophets would predict the future. One could tell if a prophet was a true prophet or a false prophet by whether his predictions came true or not (Deuteronomy 18:22). This was not the only test for a prophet, however. If a prophet led the people away from the one true God, or if he prophesied in the name of another god, he was to be put to death (see Deuteronomy 13).

The office of prophet as God's spokesman in the Old Testament was so important that the coming Messiah could be described as a prophet (see Deuteronomy 18:15–20). Both men and women could be prophets in Old Testament times.[1]

New Testament

The prophet in the New Testament seems to have a somewhat narrower job description. For example, Agabus is a prophet (Acts 21:10), but seems to limit his activity to predicting future events. Most of those who prophesy reveal future events, but not all who prophesy are true prophets (as Jesus warns in Matthew 24:11 and Mark 13:22).[2] As in the Old Testament, both women and men prophesy.[3]

Interpreting Prophecy

The modern student of the Bible needs to ask an important question when reading about prophecy: *Can a prophet, inspired by the Holy Spirit, predict the future?* In Acts 11:28, Luke records an incident where Agabus, led by the Spirit, predicted a famine. Luke also notes that this prediction was fulfilled in the reign of Claudius (who died in AD 54). The date of the prediction was approximately AD 41 (as indicated by the death of James the son of Zebedee in Acts 12). Later this same prophet, Agabus, predicts that Paul will be arrested and handed over to the Gentiles (Acts 21:10–11). His prediction is fulfilled when Paul reaches Jerusalem (Acts 21:27–36).

The testimony of God's Word in that prophecy, specifically the prediction of future events, is a gift that God gives when and where it pleases Him. Satan also "inspires" people so that they can tell something of the future (as in the case of the slave girl in Philippi, Acts 16:16–18). Yet it is only the true prophet who has the message of salvation and points people to the one true God. Thus we see that Jesus is our Prophet *par excellence* (Deuteronomy 18:18; John 6:14).

Since the few New Testament prophetic passages are fulfilled shortly after the prophecy is given (with the exception of some passages in Matthew 24–25; Mark 13; Luke 21; and Revelation—these will be covered in ch. 11), we will consider Old Testament prophecy in this chapter.

Interpretation of prophecy can be difficult. Sometimes a prophet clearly predicts a future event, quite often fulfilled centuries later in the person and work of Jesus Christ. Sometimes a prophet acts out his prophecy, like a visual aid in a children's sermon. Sometimes the New Testament sees prophetic meaning in an Old Testament event, which by itself may not seem prophetic.

Guidelines for Interpretation

We can use three guidelines to help us understand Old Testament prophecy:

- Look for the intended meaning of the prophecy.

- See if the New Testament refers to the Old Testament passage under study.
- Understand the difference between direct (verbal) prophecy and symbolic (action) prophecy.

Practicing the Guidelines

Micah 5:2

The prophet Micah lived about seven hundred years before the birth of Jesus. He warned God's people to repent of their sin, turn away from idols, and give up empty ritualism. He promised God's forgiveness to those who would turn to Him in faith and looked forward to the day when God's promised Messiah would take away the sins of the world. Read Micah 5:2 and answer the following questions:

1. Whose birth does Micah predict?
2. Where is this person to be born?
3. How important is the place of this person's birth?

In Micah 5:2, he predicts the birthplace of that Savior: the village Bethlehem in the region of Ephrathah in the tribal area occupied by Judah. This was an unimportant village in Micah's day, but because the messianic king would be born there, its historical importance would be very great. This kind of prophecy is the easiest to interpret. It contains no codes or secret messages. The message is quite plain. Sometime in the future, God's promised Messiah will be born in Bethlehem.

Jewish scholars had this same understanding of Micah 5:2 when the Magi came to Jerusalem looking for the one who had been born king of the Jews. The chief priests and teachers of the Bible, gathered by Herod the Great, knew exactly where the Messiah would be born (Matthew 2:1–6). These experts in the Old Testament even quoted Micah 5:2 to Herod. The prophecy seems very straightforward in Micah and (using the second guideline) our understanding is confirmed by Matthew in the New Testament.[4] This is the simplest form of prophecy—predicting a single event that Scripture later records as fulfilled.

Jeremiah 31:15

Sometimes New Testament writers look at Old Testament events and recognize a pattern that foreshadows an incident in the life of Jesus. We will look at two examples in the second chapter of Matthew.

In Matthew 2:18, the author cites Jeremiah 31:15 and sees a connection between that verse and the slaughter of infants at Bethlehem. The wailing of the mothers for their murdered sons fulfills (or repeats) a pattern highlighted in Jeremiah 31. Rachel, favorite wife of Jacob, had been buried near the town of Ramah. Ramah was about five miles north of Jerusalem. When Babylon conquered Jerusalem, the captives were led away on a route that passed near Ramah. Jeremiah pictures Rachel, dead for more than ten centuries, weeping for her descendants as they are taken into captivity in a foreign land (Babylon).

As we have seen before, the original context is important. Jeremiah 31:15 appears in the midst of consolation, a promise by God to bring back the captives, a message of hope and life in the midst of death and destruction. That is, of course, the same kind of situation we find in Matthew 2. In the midst of the death and destruction of the infants, the message of life and hope (Jesus Christ) shines brightly.[5]

Hosea 11:1

Matthew also sees a pattern when Jesus and His parents returned from Egypt, where they had gone to escape Herod the Great. In 2:15, Matthew quotes Hosea 11:1, "Out of Egypt I called My son." In Hosea, the prophet refers to the original exodus as he reminds his readers that God is calling them to repentance as a loving father calls a wayward son. The tragedy is that Israel did not listen to God's gracious invitation and continued in their idolatrous and sinful ways. Like them, Jesus travels from Egypt to Palestine. But unlike them, He follows the Law perfectly, the ideal Son. Jesus fulfills the pattern of Sonship and thus fulfills an action prophecy.

Jeremiah 31:31–34

Sometimes the intended meaning of a prophecy is broader than it first appears. We can use Jeremiah 31:31–34 as an example. Read this passage and answer the following:

1. To whom does God promise a new covenant?
2. How will God give them this covenant?

3. What is the essence of this new covenant?

The author of Hebrews twice quotes this passage (Hebrews 8:8–12 and 10:16–17). He makes the point that this new covenant (or testament) is superior to the covenant God made with Moses for four reasons:

1. God will write this on their hearts (minds) and not on stone tablets.
2. God will establish a personal fellowship with His people.
3. God will remove all ignorance and disobedience from His people.
4. God will forgive all sins forever.

This new testament will replace the old, the author of Hebrews says. Because this prophecy looks forward to the time when the final sacrifice for sin will have been made, the New Testament era contains no sacrificial system. Jesus makes the sacrifice once for all. As is clear in both the Old and New Testaments, God intends to include Gentiles in this new covenant. This becomes evident in Paul's understanding of the Gospel (Romans 1:16–17).[6] It is also true that this promise will not be completely fulfilled until Jesus returns, judges the living and the dead, and provides the new heavens and the new earth for His people.

The "Now" and the "Not Yet"

Living between the first and second coming of Jesus, we find ourselves in a time of joy and sorrow. We celebrate the victory of Jesus over sin, death, and the devil; yet we struggle daily with sin, fear death, and are tripped up by the devil. The end of the world has already come in the person and work of Jesus Christ; yet, somehow, we await the end of the world that is yet to come. This can create challenges for us when we interpret prophetic passages. Let's take Joel 2:28–32 as an example. Read this passage and answer the following:

1. When does God pour out His Holy Spirit?
2. When do all God's people prophesy, dream dreams, and see visions?
3. When does the sun turn to darkness and the moon to blood?
4. When will everyone who calls on the name of the Lord be saved?

We might think that the answer to all these questions is "on the Last Day." Yet Peter quotes this passage in the first Christian sermon spoken on Pentecost (Acts 2:14–26). He tells the crowd that this prophecy of Joel is fulfilled on that day, as the disciples were filled with the Holy Spirit and spoke the Gospel in languages they had not studied. We might also remember that the sun was darkened by day at Jesus' crucifixion (Matthew 27:45) and that people were raised from the dead when Jesus died (Matthew 27:52).

The next age (post-resurrection) has already begun. And yet it has not fully arrived. In a way, it's like dawn. Darkness fades as the sun begins to rise and, for about half an hour, it's almost light. This is sometimes called "false dawn." It seems like dawn, yet when the sun finally comes up, real dawn is so much brighter.

The New Testament age is a little like a false dawn. The Son has arisen, the light shines, but the full light of the Son won't be evident until His glorious return. Many Old Testament prophetic passages that look forward to the coming of the Messiah conceive of the first and second coming as though it were one event, which it is—the victory of Christ, crucified and risen!

Chapter 9 Notes

1. Prophetesses include Miriam, Moses' sister (Exodus 15:20); Deborah, judge of Israel (Judges 4:4); Huldah (2 Kings 22:14); and Isaiah's wife (Isaiah 8:3).
2. Not every person who prophesies accurately is a believer. Sometimes a person prophesies because of the office he holds, as Caiaphas did in John 11:51. Caiaphas apparently did not believe in Jesus as his Savior. Yet he prophesied because he held the office of high priest.
3. The four daughters of Philip the evangelist prophesied (Acts 21:9), and the women of Corinth were permitted to prophesy as long as they covered their heads (1 Corinthians 11:5–16).
4. Not everyone knew that Jesus was born in Bethlehem. Since He came from Nazareth in Galilee, people thought He was born there (see John 7:41–42). Being from Nazareth was not a claim to fame (as Nathanael notes in John 1:46), but even this fulfills prophecy (as Matthew records in 2:23).

5. This event is presented in very vivid and picturesque language in Revelation 12:1–5.
6. Since a covenant was "cut" by sacrificing an animal at the time it took effect, it was sealed in blood. When Jesus institutes the Lord's Supper, He draws our attention to this by saying, "This cup is the new covenant in My blood" (1 Corinthians 11:25).

Chapter 10

Parables in the Bible

WHEN WE FIRST LEARN THE BIBLE, WE OFTEN LEARN IT BY means of the stories our teachers tell us. Many of these stories are parables that Jesus told and that the Gospel writers wrote down. But parables can present a problem when we ask, "What is the intended meaning?" Unlike narrative sections of the Bible, symbolism frequently requires a reader to "decode" the story to discover the original, intended meaning.

What is a parable? Do we have any rules to help us understand them as the original storyteller intended? Why did Jesus tell parables in the first place?

Definition of a Parable

Perhaps we best define a parable in simple terms: *A parable is an earthly story with a heavenly meaning.* Although we find a few parables in the Old Testament, most biblical parables occur in the New Testament, almost all of them in the Gospels. These parables are pictures of the kingdom of God in action, with some element of mystery. The heart of a parable is comparison, but a parable is more than a comparison. The difference between a comparison and a parable may be illustrated by looking at Deuteronomy 25:4 (cited by Paul in 1 Corinthians 9:9–10 and 1 Timothy 5:17–18) and contrasting it with the parable of the mustard seed (Mark 4:30–32).

In Deuteronomy 25:4, Moses writes, "You shall not muzzle an ox when it is treading out the grain." On the surface, it seems that Moses is simply giving a humane command to people who use oxen to thresh grain.[1] However, the context (as we have seen so often) alerts us to the fact that this may not be so. The section of Deuteronomy in which 25:4 appears deals with people, not animals—particularly people who are in trouble.

Deuteronomy 25:1–3 prescribes beating as a punishment, but humanely limits the number of lashes. Deuteronomy 25:5–10 records the Levirate law, a regulation that requires a near kinsman to raise up a child for a childless, deceased relative. This ensures the continuation of the family line.

Does Moses really have oxen in mind in verse 4, or could he be using a comparison encouraging his readers to realize the need for humane treatment of people just as they humanely treat an ox while it is treading out the grain? When Paul cites this verse in 1 Corinthians and 1 Timothy, he uses it to support his position that a person has the right to make a living from preaching and teaching the Gospel. In 1 Corinthians 9:9–10, he asks, "Is it for oxen that God is concerned? Does He not certainly speak for our sake?" By the word *thresh*, Paul creates the comparison between the ox threshing and the man threshing. What do they have in common? Both hope to share the benefits of their work.

Parables, in contrast, are told or written as stories with characters, actions, and outcomes. Sometimes Jesus tells long and elaborate stories (like the parable of the prodigal son in Luke 15:11–32). At other times, His parables are quite short, as in the case of the parable of the mustard seed (Mark 4:30–32; Matthew 13:31–32; Luke 13:18–19). The kingdom of God, Jesus says, is like a mustard seed. It starts out very small and grows very large over a long period of time,[2] so large that various kinds of birds can find shade in its branches.[3]

Jesus may have had a second point of comparison in mind if He was thinking of Daniel 4:21 when He spoke this parable. In the dream that Daniel interpreted, a tree holds many kinds of birds. The tree represented a kingdom so large that it reaches "to the ends of the earth" (Daniel 4:22) and includes all kinds of people. If this is background for the parable, Jesus may be hinting that His kingdom would be open for people of all ethnic backgrounds—and not, as was often popularly thought, for Jewish people only.

Guidelines for Interpretation

We can offer a number of guidelines for interpreting parables:

1. A parable usually has one main point; any other points are secondary.
2. A parable illustrates, not establishes, doctrine. We do not use a parable to try to "prove" a doctrinal teaching.
3. A parable creates a comparison, but we should not compare every detail in every parable to something in the real world.
4. The details of a parable come from the real world. Impossible things (like talking dogs or flying pigs) do not appear in Jesus' parables. However, sometimes a parable includes an action that would be shocking and probably would never actually occur (as in the parable of the friend at midnight).
5. New Testament parables often have a real-world background, either in the Old Testament or in the history of Palestine.

The Reason for Parables

In Mark 4:10–12 (parallel passages are Matthew 13:14–15; Luke 8:10), Jesus explains the reason for parables. He has been conducting His public ministry for some time (perhaps a year or so), and opposition has begun to form (recorded in Mark 3).Thus Jesus turns to parables as a form of teaching. This prevents His enemies from interfering with His ministry of teaching, preaching, and healing. Parables are stories. How can His adversaries charge Him in ecclesiastical court (the Jewish Council) or in secular court (Pontius Pilate) with telling stories?

Read Mark 4:10–12 and answer the following:

1. To whom has the "secret" (or "mystery") of the kingdom been given?
2. Which Old Testament passage does Jesus quote?
3. What is the original context of this Old Testament passage?
4. How long will the hardness of heart last in the original context?

By means of parables, Jesus keeps His messianic status a secret, revealing it only to His disciples. At the same time, the parables both hide and reveal. They reveal spiritual truths to those in the kingdom of God—

those who believe in Jesus—and hide them from those outside the kingdom—those who do not believe in Jesus. Unbelievers may understand that some of the parables are spoken against them (as in Mark 12:12), but can do very little about it.

Jesus cites Isaiah 6:9–10, part of Isaiah's call by God to be a prophet. God lets Isaiah know that the people will reject his message, ignore his warnings, and turn their backs on both God and His prophet. God will harden their hearts until the cities lie ruined, the houses are deserted, and the land is desolated (Isaiah 6:11). Then the people will cry to God for help. This prophecy was fulfilled within twenty years.

By citing Isaiah 6:9–10, Jesus reveals the reason for using parables in His teaching ministry. Also, He hints that He will continue to speak in parables until the judgment of God is executed—that is, until He dies on the cross for the sins of the world. His messianic status and the true nature of the Kingdom (faith in Jesus as God and Lord) remain hidden until after that time.[4] After the judgment of God has been executed upon Jesus, the news of the Kingdom will be proclaimed beginning in Jerusalem, then Judea-Samaria, and even to the ends of the earth (as Jesus promises in Acts 1:8).

Practice Interpreting Parables

We will read three parables: the parable of the sower (Mark 4:1–20), the parable of the prodigal son (Luke 15:11–32), and an Old Testament parable (2 Samuel 12:1–10).

Mark 4:1–20

Read Mark 4:3–8 and answer the following:

1. What is the main point of the parable?
2. What is the background of the parable?
3. What secondary points, if any, do you find in this parable?
4. Which elements in the story represent something outside the story?

In a few parables, like this one, Jesus answers these questions (Mark 4:13–20).[5] The main point is that a person enters the kingdom of God and becomes fruitful by means of the Word. Those who reject the Word or lose it over a period of time are unfruitful. (No deeds of faith occur because they lack or lose saving faith.) Jesus uses the agriculture of the day as the background of the parable. It is similar to our own methods in some ways and different in others. The farmer scattered the seed by hand on top of the soil and then plowed it under. Scholars debate whether the average farmer would have sown seed on ground he knew to be rocky or shallow.

By sowing seed over all the ground, the farmer in the parable sows most generously, almost excessively. (Perhaps this is a secondary point: Jesus sows the Word among all types of people.) For Jesus to make His point—the purpose of the story—seed must fall on various soils. Some who hear God's Word do not believe it, and they did not put it into practice in their lives.

In this parable (and in the others that Jesus explains), each element of the story represents something in the real world. The soil represents people, the birds of the air represent Satan, the seed is the Word, the sun symbolizes persecution or trouble, and thorns reflect the deceitfulness of wealth and the desire for material goods.

Luke 15:11–32

We can easily interpret the parables Jesus explains. But what of the parables He does not explain? In Luke 15, the author records a series of three parables. He gives us the context by recording the historical situation for these three (15:1–2). Jesus tells a parable of a man who loses and then finds one of a hundred sheep. Next, Jesus relates a parable of a woman who loses and then finds one of ten coins.

Both parables contained elements that would have offended the Pharisees and their scribes (experts in Old Testament law). Shepherding was a lowly, sometimes despised profession (every shepherd worked on the Sabbath) and women did not have the same social standing as men. Jesus boldly asks His audience to think of themselves as a shepherd and then to imagine themselves as a woman, both of which would have angered the Pharisees. Jesus explicitly tells us the point in both of these parables: God wants sinners to repent and turn to Him; when they do, He gladly forgives their sins. This sets up the reader of Luke's Gospel for the third parable, a much longer story with a strong main point and a biting secondary question.

Read Luke 15:11–32 and answer the following:

1. What is the main point of the parable?
2. Why are the actions of the younger son so shocking?

3. What changes the younger son from a scheming and selfish person into someone who truly repents?
4. How does the older son reveal his attitude toward his father?
5. How does the father humiliate himself with both sons?

Jesus repeats the main point of the two preceding parables: God wants sinners to repent, and He gladly forgives them. Undoubtedly, this simple point strikes home in the heart of Jesus' audience much more forcefully than it did in the first two parables, largely due to a series of shocking and surprising events.

First, the younger son asks for his inheritance. Culturally, this was never done. That would be like asking your father to drop dead. The father's response may have been equally shocking—he gives the boy his inheritance![6] Jesus' original audience might well have expected the father in the story to disown his son and expel him from house and village, but the father simply turns over the young man's inheritance to him.

Two big questions arise about the parable. First, what changes the selfish boy into a repentant son? Second, do all the parts of the story represent something outside of the story?

The difference between verses 19 and 21 provides an opportunity to examine variations in reputable interpretations of the parable. Most traditional interpretations pretty much ignore the difference between the verses. They simply portray the son as a penitent sinner returning home.

Some Bible scholars (such as Ken Bailey, in *Finding the Lost: Cultural Keys to Luke 15* [Concordia, 1992]) argue that the words in verse 19 ("Treat me as one of your hired servants") indicate that the young man had not repented; he merely had concocted a scheme to get onto his father's payroll. In Bailey's view, the young man's only interest was to play on his father's sympathies and get a job working for him (expecting much better pay and working conditions).[7] Only after the father runs to him (men of stature did not run in that society) and so warmly welcomes him back does this young man finally repent, confessing his sin before his father without trying to get something out of him. Reconciliation, in this view, follows the Gospel (the demonstration of the father's love) rather than the Law (the decrepit condition in which the son found himself). This parable not only serves to remind us that the Bible reflects a different culture (the behavior of the father throughout the story is shocking!) but that distinguishing Law and Gospel remains a vitally important tool for the interpreter.

Moving to the second question, do all the parts of the story represent something outside of the story? That was true with the parable of the sower, but we shall find that it does not work with this parable (nor with some others), even though we sometimes try to make it work.

Given the context of Luke 15 (and the contrast between sinners and the Pharisees who considered themselves righteous[8]), we can readily see the younger son as a figure representing sinners and the older son as a character symbolizing the "righteous" Pharisees—indeed, any self-righteous person. However, we note limitations when we attempt to have the father represent God, since the story does not provide a complete picture of God. (For example, nobody dies for the sins of either son.) Regardless, the father represents a characteristic of God. God is the waiting, loving Father. He loves sinners and wants them to repent.

We dare not try to make all of the details of the story reflect some reality outside of the story. Doing so could make interpreting parables no more than an entertaining—but ultimately useless—game. What does the ring symbolize? What does the fattened calf represent? What is the "deeper meaning" of the robe or of the kiss or the fact that the father in the story put his arms around the young man's neck? What do the pigs symbolize and what symbolic value do the pods have? What is the real-world meaning of the goat that the older son complains about? We could go on and on and never get to the point that Jesus wants to make!

The younger son returns, repents, and is forgiven. His father celebrates by throwing a party, but the older brother refuses to come in. Again the father humiliates himself as he comes outside, leaving the party, to plead with his son.[9] And what happens to the older boy? Jesus leaves that to our imagination.

Jesus tells an open-ended parable that forcefully invites the Pharisees to join in the party—to rejoice with God and with His angels over the sinners that repent and are forgiven. Will they or won't they? At the time of the story, the question was still very much in doubt.

2 Samuel 12:1–10

In the third parable, an Old Testament story, we see again the importance of context. Read 2 Samuel 12:1–10 and answer the following:

1. What events lead up to this parable? (See 2 Samuel 11.)
2. Why does God send Nathan to David?

3. What was David's judgment against the rich man in Nathan's story?
4. What was the ultimate point of Nathan's parable?

The history of 2 Samuel 11 provides the background to the story in 2 Samuel 12. The author records that in the spring, when kings go off to war, David stayed home in Jerusalem and General Joab led the Israelite army against the Ammonites.[10] While home, David had an affair with the wife of one of Joab's soldiers, Uriah the Hittite. In an effort to cover up the affair, David resorts to a number of ploys to get Uriah to sleep with his wife, Bathsheba. However, God's Law specifically required that a man on active military duty refrain from marital relations. Uriah, faithful to that Law, refused to sleep with his own wife.[11] David, guilty of the capital crime of adultery,[12] conspires with his general, Joab, to have Uriah killed in battle. The problem is compounded when Joab arranges to have several soldiers killed so the murder isn't obvious.

God sends Nathan to confront David—to rebuke David for his crimes and to provide an opportunity for repentance. God intends to use the story recorded in 2 Samuel 12:1–4 to lead David to repentance. David pronounces the rich man guilty of a crime deserving death. However, since the Law does not allow that, David fines the rich man the price of the sheep times four.

Nathan sums up his point neatly in the direct address, "You are the man!" (2 Samuel 12:7).[13] By means of this parable, David realizes that he has sinned against God and makes his confession (2 Samuel 12:13; see also Psalms 32 and 51).

To interpret this parable, we need not figure out what the poor man represents, what the rich man symbolizes, what the rich man's guests stand for, or the significance of the ewe. The details of the parable do not line up with the specific details of David's actions. If the details of the parable corresponded to the details of history, the poor man in the parable would be murdered and the ewe lamb stolen by the rich man to be added to his already impressive flock.

These facts remind us of how important it is to recognize that parables generally have one main point. Sometimes the details of parables are symbolic (like the parable of the sower), but most of the time, as with Nathan's parable, they are not. Nathan's story in chapter 12 has one thing in common with David's history in chapter 11: a man who had much violated the rights of a man who had little, taking what was another man's for his own.

Final Guidelines

What have we learned in our practice session of interpreting parables?

1. Context is important; always read the material before and after the unit under study.
2. Understanding the background of the parables is helpful. Culture, history, geography, and the like differ markedly from our own.
3. Sometimes we need to use various tools for Bible study in order to get the point. (These tools will be listed in ch. 12.)

Chapter 10 Notes

1. A good Bible encyclopedia will help the modern city dweller understand this ancient agricultural practice. Chapter 12 will discuss various tools for Bible study, including an encyclopedia.
2. Based on Malachi 3:1, which predicts that the Messiah will appear suddenly in the temple, most people expected the messianic kingdom to come rapidly once the Messiah publicly declared Himself. The parable of the mustard seed is a strong contrast to this popular expectation.
3. This is an example of the classic argument "from the lesser to the greater." If something is true in the case of a lesser thing, how much more true is it in the case of a greater thing!
4. Jesus anticipates this in Matthew 10:27 and specifically commands silence regarding His messianic kingship in Matthew 16:20 and 17:9.
5. Other parables where Jesus explains the meaning of the story include the parable of the net (Matthew 13:47–50) and the parable of the weeds (Matthew 13:24–30, 36–43).
6. The younger son got one third of the inheritance; the older brother got two thirds. The law of primogeniture (the law of the firstborn) was that he receive a double portion of the

inheritance (Deuteronomy 21:17). Daughters would receive an inheritance if a man had no son (Numbers 36).

7. After all, how low could a Jewish boy go? He was feeding the pigs of Gentiles.
8. Remember that "righteous" describes a person who keeps his end of the bargain—in this case, God's Law.
9. This would have been most shocking to Jesus' original listeners.
10. Spring was the beginning of the warm, dry season. It is not clear why David remained at the palace instead of leading his army.
11. Note the irony in the fact that the foreigner, Uriah, is ultimately faithful to the covenant, while the covenant king, David, a man after God's own heart (as he is called in 1 Samuel 13:14 and Acts 13:22), proves unfaithful.
12. Adultery (that is, having intercourse with another man's wife) is a crime that God specifically forbids in Leviticus 20:10 and Deuteronomy 22:22. The Law punished this sin by the execution of both parties.
13. Usually, kings in the Near East could not be approached so casually. For example, Esther takes her life in her hands when she speaks to the king of Persia, her husband, without first being invited to do so. The king of God's people, bound by the covenant, is here held accountable to his King, the Lord, for what he has done.

Chapter 11

Apocalyptic Writings

ONE COULD COMPARE THE ART OF INTERPRETATION WITH playing various card games with the same deck of cards. We could play rummy or we could play solitaire with the same deck but with different rules. So it is with different types of literature—straightforward historical sections call for sticking with the plain and obvious meaning of the text. Apocalyptic prophecies require a slightly different set of rules that take into consideration the codes the author uses.

As exciting as it might be to attempt to interpret Revelation, it is better to begin a lifetime of Bible study elsewhere. We need to learn to walk before trying to run. If we begin our study with apocalyptic prophecy, we may frequently read our own ideas into the text (a very popular game) and make believe that the original writer had our thoughts in mind.

The term *apocalyptic* comes from a Greek word that means "unveiled"; "revealed." Imagine the day of dedication for a new statue in a town park. A large cover is draped over the figure. As the crowd gathers in anticipation, the covering is slowly lifted. The base, the middle, then the whole statue is revealed. That's what "apocalyptic" writings do. They lift the veil from the future so that everyone can see clearly what lies ahead.

It may seem ironic that apocalyptic writings almost always use codes: numbers are often symbolic, colors may have meaning, and powerful visions of very strange creatures abound. In chapter 2, our study of interpretation showed us that we need to stick to the plain meaning of the text. In apocalyptic writings, we replace that principle with a different guide: **Know the code!**

Apocalyptic Writing in the Ancient World

Apocalyptic writings were quite common in the ancient world, particularly from the second century before Jesus through the second century after His death and resurrection. Quite a number of nonscriptural apocalyptic books were written during these four centuries: 1 Enoch, 2 Baruch, 4 Ezra (also known as 2 Esdras), 3 Baruch, Apocalypse of Abraham, and others.

Perhaps you have never heard of these books, much less read them. Scripture never mentions and rarely quotes these apocalypses. In the Book of Jude, the author quotes 1 Enoch 1:9 (in vv. 14–15) and refers to a story in the Assumption of Moses in verse 9. Quotations of works outside the Bible are not limited to apocalypses. In Titus 1:12, Paul quotes Epimenides, in Acts 17:18 he cites Aratus, and in 2 Peter 2:22 Peter cites a proverb popularized in the ancient story of Ahikar. Thus, when Jude cites a book outside of the Bible with which his readers would have been familiar, he is following in the footsteps of Peter and Paul.

Apocalyptic Writing in the Bible

The longest apocalyptic part of the Bible is the Revelation of Jesus Christ to John. Strictly speaking, Revelation is not an apocalypse but a prophecy that uses apocalyptic imagery. Revelation lacks a number of features common to true apocalypses. (For example, the author does not claim to be a great figure from the past, such as Enoch or Moses, but identifies himself as John.) John calls his book *a prophecy* (Revelation 1:3; 10:11; 22:7, 10). He then proceeds to reveal the events of the New Testament era, culminating in the final judgment and in the advent of the new heaven and new earth.

John's message, like the message of other apocalyptic prophecies of the Bible, assures us that Jesus conquers Satan in the end. No matter what persecution a Christian faces, we must remain faithful to Jesus because He (and only He) will give the crown of life to the one who faithfully endures persecution (as He promises in Revelation 2:10).

We also find apocalyptic prophecies in Joel, Ezekiel, Zechariah (chs. 9–14), Isaiah (chs. 24–27), and Daniel (chs. 7–12). Some writers call the parts of the Gospels where Jesus talks about the destruction of Jerusalem and the end of the world apocalyptic, or the "little apocalypse" (Matthew 24–25; Mark 13; Luke 21). Since we try to base our doctrine on clear, unambiguous passages of Scripture, we usually do not base our teachings on apocalyptic sections. These portions of Scripture tend to play a supportive rather than a foundational role in establishing our teachings.

Guidelines for Understanding Apocalyptic Writing

When we do read apocalyptic sections, three things are very helpful:

1. **Keep the clear parts of Scripture in view.** Like ancient sailors who keep the coastline in view, we do well to have "control chapters" so we don't get lost in apocalyptic writing. For Revelation, it's a good idea to keep Matthew 24–25 in our mind's eye.
2. **Understand the outline.** Know how the smaller parts fit together to make up the whole. In Revelation, for example, we have an introduction (ch. 1) and a conclusion (20:11–22:21) with seven units between them. Several of these units overlap (the seven seals, 6:1–8:5; the seven trumpets, 8:6–11:19; and the seven bowls, 15:1–16:21) and describe the same period of time but with a growing emphasis on the end of time. Some people take each section as referring to a successive period of time and thus misunderstand John's point.
3. **Know the code.** Colors and numbers have meaning.[1] Red and black are generally bad; white is good. Three denotes God and four refers to creation. Seven equals fullness and ten indicates completeness. Thus, 144,000 dressed in white (Revelation 7 and 14) equals the complete number of people who are saved by grace through faith in Jesus Christ. Their sins are forgiven and they are credited with Jesus' good works (thus, they wear white) and not one believer is missing. God's people (3 x 4 = 12) from both Old and New Testament times (12 x 12 = 144), the complete number God has saved by faith (10 cubed = 1,000) are represented by the number *144,000* (144 x 1,000).[2] Using numbers in this way seems strange to us, but it does not take long to grasp John's meaning once we know the code.

Remember, though, that not all numbers in the Bible are symbolic. For example, the number *153* has no hidden meaning when Peter catches 153 fish (John 21:11). He simply caught a large number of sizable fish.

Practicing the Guidelines

Let's read Revelation 20:1–3 and answer the following questions:

1. Who is the angel in 20:1?
2. What might the chain in 20:1 represent?
3. Who is the dragon in 20:2?
4. How long is the dragon chained?
5. For what purpose is the dragon chained?

Normally, we think of angels as spirit-beings without bodies, although they can take physical forms when it pleases God.[3] The Greek word for angel (*angelos*) means "messenger." It can sometimes refer to people (as it does in Luke 7:24).

Given the description in Revelation 10 and also here in Revelation 20, the angel might well be Jesus. The picture of the angel in 20:1 is consistent with Jesus. He descended from heaven in the incarnation, possesses the keys of the kingdom of God (Matthew 16:19), and has the power to cast demons into hell (Luke 8:31, which uses the same word for hell—*abyss*). Jesus is also the one who told the parable of the stronger man binding the strong man and then ransacking the strong man's house (Luke 11:21–22). We normally take this figure of speech to refer to Jesus overthrowing Satan's reign on earth and saving sinners from Satan's bondage.

If this identification is correct (that the angel of 20:1 is Jesus), then the chain might symbolize the Holy Spirit. The Church was "born" on Pentecost with the outpouring of the Holy Spirit (Acts 2), and Paul talks about a restraining force on Satan (2 Thessalonians 2:6–7) during the New Testament age.[4] Further, Jesus talks of the Father sending Him and, in His name, sending the Spirit. This interpretation seems to be supported by the fact in Scripture that only God Himself is more powerful than Satan. Even the archangel Michael refers Satan to God rather than rebuking Satan himself (Jude 9).

Our answer to the first two questions may seem a bit tenuous, but we find that we cannot easily make hard-and-fast, solid identification of apocalyptic images. The better you know the rest of Scripture, the more readily you can identify apocalyptic figures.

The third question is much easier. The figure of a dragon appears for the first time in Revelation 12:3 and occurs a total of twelve times in the book. This character cannot be anyone but the chief of the fallen angels.

The text says that he is chained for a thousand years. But how long is that? Numbers in Revelation are consistently symbolic, and that is the case here. One thousand represents the complete time God has set aside for the Gentile mission—that is, for Gospel outreach to the nations (Matthew 24:14); 10 cubed = 1,000, a symbol for the New Testament era.

Some object to this interpretation. They maintain that, since evil still seems to be present in the world, it is impossible to think that Satan is bound. Therefore, they say, these one thousand years must refer to a literal reign of Jesus before Judgment Day. As we read all of Revelation 20:3, however, we find that John does not say Satan is bound so that he cannot do anything at all. Rather, John says that Satan is bound so that he cannot deceive the nations (the Gentiles) anymore. In other words, Satan cannot stop the Gospel's success.

The story of Jesus and His crucifixion and resurrection will go out from Jerusalem to the four corners of the earth, and people will be brought into the kingdom of God's grace. Satan, try as he might, cannot stop this. Spreading this Gospel news is the purpose of the New Testament era and the job description of the Church. Jesus promises that not even the gates of hell will prevail against the Church in her mission (Matthew 16:18). At the end of the New Testament age, Satan will be released for a short time, and then the end of the world will come.

This same message of hope and confidence appears in Revelation 11. There, two witnesses (representing the Church)[5] evangelize for 1,260 days—three and a half years—and cannot be harmed.[6] After their time of witness ends, they are killed, and their bodies lie in the street for three and a half days, after which they stand up and the judgment of the world commences.[7]

Several things become quickly apparent as we interpret apocalyptic writing:

- The better we know the rest of Scripture, the better we are able to interpret apocalyptic prophecies in the Bible.

- The better we know the apocalyptic prophecy, the more likely we are to understand a particular passage or paragraph as the author intended it.

Chapter 11 Notes

1. A good resource for this is Bruce M. Metzger, *Breaking the Code: Understanding the Book of Revelation* (Nashville: Abingdon Press, 1993).
2. It is very important that your Bible translate the numbers as they appear in Revelation rather than convert them to modern equivalents. Revelation 14:20 speaks of 1,600 stadia, a Roman unit of distance. If a translation uses a number other than 1,600 when converting to a modern equivalent (e.g., "about 200 miles"), it loses part of John's message. That message is contained in the number *1,600*, not in the distance. 1,600 = all of creation (4 x 4 x 10 x 10).
3. Sometimes these forms are human, as in the resurrection and ascension accounts, and sometimes they are quite bizarre, as in Revelation 4 and Ezekiel 1.
4. Greek nouns have gender (masculine, feminine, neuter) like German and many other languages. The gender of the restraining force in 2 Thessalonians 2:6 is neuter, and the gender of the restraining force in 2 Thessalonians 2:7 is masculine. The word *Spirit* in Greek is neuter, and yet the Holy Spirit is a person in the Trinity. The alternation between neuter and masculine might reflect this, or the one who restrains in verse 7 might refer to Jesus.
5. Strong echoes from Zechariah and Ezekiel show up in Revelation 11.
6. Like Elijah in 1 Kings 17, they stop the rain. In 2 Kings 1, fire consumes their enemies.
7. This is very similar to material in Daniel, especially chapters 7 and 12. Metzger, *Breaking the Code* (p. 13), points out that of the 404 verses in Revelation, 278 contain one or more references to the Old Testament.

Chapter 12

Bible Tools for Better Bible Study

WHEN WE PICK UP OUR BIBLES, WE BEGIN AN ADVENTURE. When we open our Bibles, we open the door to a world very different from our own in many ways.

Human nature has not changed since Adam and Eve rebelled against God in Genesis 3, but almost everything else about the people and places in the Bible is different from our world. Each of the books of the Bible was written by a real person (or, in some cases, people). That person lived and died in a specific culture and a particular geography with a history and a language that seem quite strange to us today. Yet God inspired these authors, moving them to write these books—for our salvation.[1]

On the one hand, the basic message of Scripture is simple: "Believe in the Lord Jesus Christ, and you will be saved" (Acts 16:31). On the other hand, much of what God says to us can be lost through ignorance of the original language and historical context. What tools can help us as we begin the adventure of Bible study?

The Original Languages

As we will see in the next chapter, the Bible was originally written in three languages: Hebrew, Aramaic,[2] and Greek. The Aramaic portions are quite small (some of Ezra and several chapters in Daniel), so that most who study the original languages study only Hebrew and Greek. These original languages are the inspired text of Scripture.

Our English translations, however, are quite good. Bible students who do not work with the original languages can be confident that they have a reasonably accurate rendition of the text.

Nonetheless, most people who have the time and self-discipline can learn the biblical languages. Since learning any language is much easier with a teacher, a Bible student who can travel to a seminary may wish to check whether the seminary offers language instruction to interested parties.

Though not as effective as class instruction for most, a computer program also can provide language instruction. Instruction in both Hebrew and Greek is available. If you have access to the Internet, you can do a search for Greek or Hebrew learning programs. Also, a number of text and workbook courses are available as well as an iTunes course based on *Fundamental Greek Grammar* by James W. Voelz (Concordia, 2014).

God's Word is effective whether in the original language or in translation. We can compare the difference between knowing the original language and a translation with two television sets—one a 12-inch black-and-white model with rabbit ears and the other a 60-inch high definition set with excellent cable or satellite reception. The detail and color are much better on the high definition TV, but you get the same plot line and characters on both sets.

Whether you study the Bible in the original languages or in translation, the same God reveals our sin and our Savior, Jesus Christ. A Bible student who works exclusively with translations may purchase an edition of the Bible that puts various translations in parallel columns. (We will discuss various modern translations in chapter 15.) A similar tool can be found on Bible Gateway (www.biblegateway.com).

Concordances

A concordance lists the Bible passages in which a particular word appears. A complete concordance—which lists *all* the passages in which the word appears—is available in large books or computer programs. Many Bibles contain smaller concordances, such as the ones in the *The Catholic Study Bible* (Oxford, 2011), *Concordia Self-Study Bible* (Concordia, 1986), *The ESV Study Bible* (Crossway, 2008), *The Lutheran Study Bible* (Concordia, 2009), and others that list only selected passages.

Obviously, a concordance becomes a very helpful tool for word studies. However, one needs to be aware that a single Hebrew or Greek term can be translated by a variety of English terms. Therefore the word study in translations may not yield the same results as word studies in the original languages. Furthermore, each translation might use a different English word to translate the same original term so that the translations seem to disagree with each other.

For example, the Greek word *sozein* can be translated *to save* in the sense of "to rescue from God's wrath on Judgment Day." It also can be translated *to be healed*; *made well* in the sense of being saved from a disease. In Mark 6:53–56, the evangelist records that Jesus was in Gennesaret and that sick people touched His garment and "were healed" (NIV, NRSV). However, the ESV and the NKJV translates this "made well." If you are doing a concordance search, you might have a difficult time finding all the passages that speak of Jesus healing people unless you know all the ways in which the Greek word *sozein* is translated in that particular version. The problem is compounded by the fact that not only can one Hebrew or Greek word be translated by a variety of English terms, but one English word can be used to translate several different Hebrew or Greek terms.

Still, a concordance is a valuable tool for Bible study. It keeps the student in the Bible itself rather than giving opinions about the Bible (primary versus secondary research). *Strong's Exhaustive Concordance of the Bible* (Hendrickson, 2007) and *Young's Analytical Concordance to the Bible* (Hendrickson, 1984) are both excellent Bible tools. Computer concordances are even more impressive and easier to use (once the student becomes familiar with them) but are far more expensive. Logos, Accordance, and BibleWorks are all very useful options. These software programs offer a multitude of features not found in books. A student who considers buying one of these should consider carefully which features in the software are really needed.

Bible Handbooks

A Bible handbook introduces the reader to the world of Holy Scripture as well as an overview of the books and their history of transmission. *Halley's Bible Handbook* has been helping students of Scripture for many years and is now in its twenty-fifth edition (Zondervan, 2007). More recently, *Concordia's Complete Bible Handbook*, second edition (Concordia, 2013) has been published. It offers a wealth of background information, maps and charts, overviews that prove very valuable to modern Bible readers, and a Bible dictionary that doubles as an index.

Bible Dictionaries and Encyclopedias

Bible dictionaries are usually one-volume books, and encyclopedias may come as multivolume sets. A dictionary lists words found in the Bible (including proper names) and gives a thumbnail sketch for that entry. A Bible dictionary is a handy tool for gathering all the pertinent data about a particular topic in the Bible. *The New Unger's Bible Dictionary* (Moody, 2006) and *Easton's Bible Dictionary* (originally published by Thomas Nelson in 1897 and now available in various formats) are both popular. (Unger is also responsible for a popular handbook to the Bible.) The following example from *Easton's Bible Dictionary* shows what a Bible dictionary does. The following information appears under the entry "Abishag":

> Father of (i.e., "given to") error, a young woman of Shunem, distinguished for her beauty. She was chosen to minister to David in his old age. She became his wife (1 Kings 1:3, 4, 15). After David's death Adonijah persuaded Bathsheba, Solomon's mother, to entreat the king to permit him to marry Abishag. Solomon suspected in this request an aspiration to the throne, and therefore caused him to be put to death. (1 Kings 2:17–25)

For comparison, *Nave's Topical Bible* (Thomas Nelson, 1979) has a much shorter entry under "Abishag":

> Wife of David, 1Ki 1:1–4; 2:13–25

A Bible encyclopedia is generally longer (three to five volumes) and includes more pictures. It may have more topics than a dictionary and may cover broader topics (e.g., "marriage" covers pp. 92–102 of volume 4 in *The Zondervan Pictorial Encyclopedia of the Bible* [Zondervan, 1975]). Bible dictionaries and encyclopedias are very helpful tools for Bible study. They help the student get an overview of a particular subject and also help the student learn background information.

Commentaries

A commentary is a verse-by-verse interpretation and explanation of Scripture. There are some one-volume Bible commentaries, but by virtue of their size, they are able to offer only limited comments (if any) on a particular Bible passage.

More thorough commentaries limit themselves to one or two books of the Bible at a time. Most commentary series are designed for pastors and Bible teachers, but (thankfully) a number are available for the lay student. The People's Bible Commentary (NIV, Concordia) is a series of paperback commentaries that provide a valuable source of help for the average and beginning Bible student. The Tyndale Commentary series (various translations, InterVarsity Press) is a similar series written at a more advanced level. The Reformation Heritage Bible Commentary series is a New Testament series underway from Concordia Publishing House, featuring both the English Standard Version and King James Version Bible text in parallel columns, with commentary on the ESV translation.

Study Bibles

A good study Bible will probably get more use than the rest of these tools combined. However, a word of caution is in order. All study Bibles reflect the doctrine of their editors and publishers. Therefore it is important to choose a study Bible that is doctrinally dependable. For example, the *Concordia Self-Study Bible* contains introductory material, helpful footnotes, outlines, charts, graphs, and a limited concordance. More recently published, *The Lutheran Study Bible* includes both study material as well as devotional content. For Reformed Christians, *The ESV Study Bible* is a popular choice. *The Catholic Study Bible* is likewise a high-quality publication. It is good to remember that reading the Holy Scripture is never merely an intellectual or academic activity but always a spiritual experience as well. Be on your guard—not all study Bibles are created equal. Some study Bibles, such as the Scofield and Ryrie study Bibles, reflect milliennialist beliefs. (Chapter 11 showed how this grows out of an erroneous interpretation of apocalyptic writing.)

Bible Atlas

A Bible atlas offers the student maps and geographical information (often including climate, history, and archaeology) about the places in the Bible. The *Crossway ESV Bible Atlas* by John Currid and David Barrett (2010) is just one example of the many atlases available to the reader of Scripture. The *Oxford Bible Atlas*, fourth edition (2007), includes material for the Apocrypha and intertestamental period. "A picture is worth a thousand words," as we know.

Other Books

Several other Bible aids may prove useful. These include *Chronological and Background Charts of the Old Testament* (1994) and *Chronological and Background Charts of the New Testament* (2009) by Zondervan. Both are very useful, putting much information at the student's fingertips. Andrew Steinmann's *From Abraham to Paul: A Biblical Chronology* (Concordia, 2011) provides dates for all dateable events in the Bible as well as how the dates were calculated. (It is the basis for the chronology in appendix two of this book.) Everett Ferguson's *Backgrounds of Early Christianity* (Eerdmans, 2003) provides some of the best background about the New Testament world. Kenneth E. Bailey has made many valuable contributions to our understanding of the world of the New Testament. *Poet & Peasant And Through Peasant Eyes*, combined edition (Eerdmans, 1983), really is indispensable for reading parables. More recently, *Jesus Through Middle Eastern Eyes* (IVP Academic, 2008) offers a broader look at the Gospels. Bailey helps modern readers sweep away misconceptions about the stories in the Gospels, bringing the ancient world to life in the text of Scripture. In addition to all these resources, new books and software become available on a regular basis. Check your bookstore (real or virtual) every so often to see what new tools are available.

A Note of Caution

Every Bible tool (except for concordances) reflects the theology and outlook of the people who produced them. Take the time, if possible, to find out something about the author, editor, or publisher of a particular book. We need to be careful not to believe everything we read. The Bible itself is the only real authority; everything else is either faithfully or unfaithfully derived from Scripture.

As we have worked through several passages in parts one and two of this book, we have used various Bible tools to interpret particular passages. Sometimes the Bible passage under study required working with the original language. A beginning student of the Bible should not feel intimidated by problems that require more expertise than the student has, but the student should be willing to ask for help when it is needed. Pastors and other experienced Bible teachers do not know all the answers, but they can often steer the beginner in the right direction. Remember, though, that only the Bible is the authority; everything else has authority derived from the Bible or is mere opinion.

Chapter 12 Notes

1. Paul makes this point in 1 Corinthians 10:1–13 when he talks about the lesson we must learn from the Hebrews during the exodus.
2. Aramaic looks like Hebrew in modern editions of the Hebrew Scriptures. At the risk of over simplification, Aramaic is to Hebrew as German is to English—similar in appearance, but different languages nonetheless.

Part Three
How We Got The Bible

The Bible is a library of many books written primarily in Hebrew and Greek over numerous centuries. Each of the two major parts, the Old Testament and the New Testament, contains different categories of books, such as history, poetry, and prophecy. Chapters 13 and 14 explore the Old Testament and the New Testament to describe how they relate to one another.

If you cannot read the languages in which the Bible was originally written, you will read the Bible in a translation or a paraphrase. This is the topic of chapter 15.

Some ancient books and writings outside the Bible help us understand the messages of Scripture. In chapter 16, you will learn about some of those writings.

Chapter 13

The Old Testament

WE DO NOT KNOW EXACTLY WHEN WRITING WAS FIRST INvented. The oldest obvious writing samples that still exist today date from around 3100 BC. They come from Sumeria, a land between the Tigris and Euphrates rivers in modern Iraq. Egyptian writings from about the same time have also survived.

Our earliest Hebrew writing is perhaps a school boy's writing exercises from the tenth century BC. This student used a clay tablet to list the months of the year and their agricultural significance. It was found in the town of Gezer and is known as the Gezer calendar. Several other archaeological finds have produced examples of Hebrew writing from the eighth century BC onward.[1]

The earliest surviving copy of the Hebrew Scriptures, however, was written much later. Until the discovery of the Dead Sea Scrolls in 1947, the oldest copy of the entire Old Testament in Hebrew that survived had been produced about AD 1000. The Dead Sea Scrolls included a large number of Hebrew Scriptures, about 95 percent of which matched the Hebrew Old Testament as we have it today. These Hebrew Scriptures must have been written down no later than the first century AD, getting us almost a thousand years closer than before to the originals, which is why the Dead Sea Scrolls were such an important discovery.

Authors and Date of Writing

The debate over who wrote the books of the Old Testament and when they were written has raged for more than two centuries. Although tradition plays a role in answering these questions, Scripture itself makes noteworthy statements about authorship and date.

We will examine the first five books of the Bible, sometimes called the Pentateuch. According to several passages (Exodus 24:4; 34:27–28; Deuteronomy 4:13; 5:22; 10:4; and others), Moses wrote at least part of the Pentateuch. Jesus states that Moses wrote this section of Scripture in Mark 10:5 and Matthew 19:8, referring to Deuteronomy 24:1–4. When the Sadducees refer to the Levirate marriage law as having come from Moses (Mark 12:19; parallels are Matthew 22:24; Luke 20:28), Jesus does not correct them.

The internal testimony of Scripture clearly shows that Moses wrote at least some of the first five books of the Bible. Some parts may have been updated later so they would be easier for a later audience to understand (see Genesis 14:14; 36:31; 47:11 where there are references to later history), and the last chapter of Deuteronomy, which records Moses' death, may have been added by someone else. However, it is fair to say that as far as the record of Scripture is concerned, Moses is the author and compiler of the Pentateuch. Since the exodus may be dated to 1446 BC (see 1 Kings 6:1), this would mean the first five books of the Bible were written in the last half of the fifteenth century BC.[2] The events that took place prior to Moses' birth in Exodus 1 would have come down to Moses, most probably in oral form. However, some written records, especially from the time of Abraham (about 2000 BC), could have been part of the resources available to Moses. (At least five different writing systems were available to Abraham. He may well have been familiar with at least one of them.)

It might seem to us that oral transmission is not very reliable. However, people who cannot read or write—or who do very little reading or writing—depend on their memories much more than we do. The human mind is capable of memorizing a large amount of information without writing of any kind, as any child under the age of 5 demonstrates. Further, the first eleven chapters of Genesis seem to be designed to be memorized for later repetition. Certain patterns of speech, narrative organization, and even word counts can ensure that the story is remembered and passed on exactly as received. Hence, the task for Moses is very realistic, even without considering divine revelation.

Thus, Moses received both oral and written accounts of the events recorded in Genesis 1–Exodus 1. He included these accounts in his history of the exodus and the Sinai wanderings, writing the books of Genesis through Deuteronomy. After the death of Moses, Joshua[3] (or someone else) likely recorded Deuteronomy 34.

Over the next one thousand years, the Holy Spirit moved people to write down the history of Israel, the poetry of its musicians, the proverbs of its wise men, and the Law and Gospel of its prophets.

The Israelites divided their Bible into three sections: the Law (Torah, the five books of Moses), the Prophets, and the Writings. The Prophets were divided into history (the Former Prophets—Joshua through 2 Kings) and prophecy (the Latter Prophets—Isaiah through Malachi). The books of 1 and 2 Chronicles were included in the category "Writings." These were the last books of the Hebrew canon (the list of books that are accepted as Holy Scripture).

Some of the books of the Old Testament name their authors (e.g., most of the prophetic books) while others are anonymous (e.g., the books of Samuel and Kings). Some books are compilations of many writers (e.g., Psalms and Proverbs), and other books name their author by a kind of pen name (e.g., the author of Ecclesiastes is identified as *Qoheleth*, "the preacher").

Some dates are very easy to fix because of historical references contained in them (e.g., the visions of Ezekiel can usually be dated with certainty to the month, day, and year), while we cannot even determine the century in which others were written (e.g., Job).We can say, though, that over the period from the fifteenth century BC through the fourth century BC a variety of people wrote prose and poetry, prophecies and wisdom. God's people recognized these writings as special. They preserved them, read and studied them, and even died for them in times of persecution.

The Old Testament in the New Testament

Jesus held the Old Testament in very high regard. His use of it shows how highly He thought of the Hebrew Scriptures. When facing Satan in the wilderness, Jesus used Scripture to fight him. Jesus quoted from the part of the Old Testament that records the temptations Israel faced during forty years in the wilderness. As Jesus finished His forty days in the wilderness, He cited Deuteronomy 8:3; 6:13, 16 (see Matthew 4:1–11; a parallel is Luke 4:1–13).

Later, in Matthew 16:4, Jesus refers to the prophet Jonah, an apparent reference to His own coming death, burial, and resurrection. In Matthew 19:3–12, He refers to Genesis 1:27 and 2:24, all in reference to an issue raised by the Pharisees in light of Deuteronomy 24:1–4. Jesus cites Psalm 8:2 in defense of the children's praise at His triumphal entry into Jerusalem (Matthew 21:16). When Jesus quotes the first verse of Psalm 110 during the last week of His earthly ministry (Matthew 22:44), He says the Holy Spirit inspired David to write the psalm (Matthew 22:43). Even in His most extreme suffering on the cross, Jesus quotes Scripture. Both Matthew and Mark record the fact that Jesus cites Psalm 22:1, a psalm of the righteous sufferer, during the crucifixion (Matthew 27:46; Mark 15:34).

The authors of the New Testament have the same high regard for the Old Testament as does Jesus. Even though Jesus and the New Testament writers often quote from the Greek translation of the Hebrew Scriptures (known as the Septuagint), they treat these Scriptures as the authoritative, inspired Word of God.[4] This is very helpful for us, because it confirms the fact that the Word of God is not bound to the original languages but remains the Word of God even in translation.

The Old Testament Canon

As stated earlier in this chapter, the canon is the list of books that are accepted as Holy Scripture. The Old Testament canon was fairly well fixed by the time of the New Testament (the first century AD), though some books of the Hebrew canon were discussed by rabbis at Jamnia (or Yavneh, near Jerusalem) around AD 100.[5]

At this gathering, the status of several books was discussed, including the Song of Solomon and Ecclesiastes. These books had apparently been considered Scripture for some time, but various features about each of these works may have troubled some rabbis. Some discussion over a few books continued in Jewish tradition. It seems, though, that by the first century AD the thirty-nine books of the Old Testament were well established as Holy Scripture and had been considered such for some time.

Summary and Conclusions

The writing of the Old Testament took place over about one thousand years. We cannot determine how many authors were involved. The time span covered in the Old Testament books ranges from the beginning of the world through the beginning of the fourth century BC. As far as we know, none of the originals of any of the books has survived. The Dead Sea Scrolls contain some copies of the Hebrew Scriptures that date to the first and second centuries BC.

Jesus and the authors of the New Testament regarded the Hebrew Scriptures as God's Word and understood that these Scriptures were written for our learning (Romans 15:4). The Old Testament is much longer than the New Testament. It includes a great deal of genealogies, history, geography, and regulations about the temple and ancient Jewish worship. Yet the Old Testament continues to point to Jesus Christ (John 5:39).

Chapter 13 Notes

1. These include the Siloam Inscription, describing the completion of a tunnel in Jerusalem from about 705 BC, and the Lachish Letters, communiqués from Lachish to Jerusalem from about 587 BC. For a more complete listing of ancient texts relating to the Old Testament, see page 5 of the *Concordia Self-Study Bible.*
2. Many scholars argue that the exodus took place in the thirteenth century BC. However, the more conservative and traditional date of the fifteenth century BC still has a large number of defenders (as in *The Lutheran Study Bible*, p. xcvi).
3. We know that Joshua could write because we know he wrote in public on at least two occasions (Joshua 8:32 and 24:26).
4. This is true even when the Septuagint is a little different from the Hebrew text. A good example is Genesis 2:24, which is cited four times in the New Testament (Matthew 19:5; Mark 10:7–8; 1 Corinthians 6:16; and Ephesians 5:31). The Hebrew text of Genesis 2:24 reads "*they* shall become one flesh," whereas the Septuagint reads "*the two* shall become one flesh."
5. See the *Lutheran Bible Companion* (St. Louis: Concordia, 2014), 2:9.

Chapter 14

The New Testament

THE NEW TESTAMENT IS A MUCH SHORTER COLLECTION OF books and took considerably less time to write than the Old Testament. The earliest New Testament work, either 1 Thessalonians or Galatians, was written about AD 51.[1] The last book, Revelation, appeared near the end of the first century AD. Thus, while the Old Testament may have taken about a thousand years to write, the New Testament was written over only fifty years or so. Many of the letters of Paul and the Epistle of James were probably written first. Matthew, Mark, and Luke wrote their Gospels sometime between AD 50 and 60. Hebrews, 1 Peter, and 2 Peter may also have been written in the sixties. Very likely, John wrote his Gospel, his Epistles, and Revelation later in the first century AD.

The New Testament Canon

The canon of the New Testament (the list of books considered to be Holy Scripture) was shaped by several factors: to know about Jesus and His teachings, to fight heresy and persecution, and to use in worship services. Ultimately, as with the Old Testament, the books that became the New Testament impressed their readers as being different, special, and having the "ring of truth" about them. Most of the New Testament books are connected to an apostle as well (Mark is associated with Peter, Luke with Paul).[2]

The Early Christian Church did not "decide" what books were authoritative, but they did recognize the unique nature of the works that we know as the New Testament. In his Easter letter to his congregations in AD 367, Bishop Athanasius of Alexandria, Egypt, listed the twenty-seven New Testament books as "divine" and called them "springs of salvation." In AD 397, at Carthage in North Africa, a church council met (with Augustine in attendance) and confirmed the canon of the New Testament. After that, very little significant discussion about which books belonged in the Bible took place until Reformation times. The Holy Spirit, who inspired the writers of Scripture, also guided the Christian Church to identify which books are, in fact, part of the canon.

Inspiration and Inerrancy

In the Bible, God reveals Himself to people. He speaks honestly and bluntly about our problem (sin) and His solution (Christ crucified). He speaks the truth to us, both in the severity of the Law and the sweetness of the Gospel.

If the Bible is merely a human record of observations, meditations, and pious thoughts about God, we would expect errors of various sorts (historical, geographical, scientific, and the like). If it is truly God's Word, we would expect accuracy in both these smaller matters and the larger issues (such as the nature of God and the relationship between Him and us). We believe the original writings (called autographs) were inerrant—that is, contained no error of any sort[3]—for the Lord says that He does not lie (Numbers 23:19; Titus 1:2).

We also believe that Scripture is inspired; that is, that God is responsible for writing it. Inspiration differs from dictation, which involves someone dictating words to a person who simply writes them down word for word. Inspiration does not work quite so simply. Read Luke 1:1–4 and answer the following:

1. Is Luke an eyewitness of the events in his Gospel?
2. How did other writers get their information?
3. How did Luke get his information?
4. Where did Luke get the information in Luke 1 and 2?
5. Does Luke claim to write a strictly chronological account?

Luke is an eyewitness to some of the events in the second volume of his work (Acts),[4] but he is not present at the events he records in the Gospel of Luke. Luke would have had a number of resources available to him, including eyewitnesses (such as Peter and other apostles) and the Jerusalem archives (e.g., the Apostolic Decree of Acts 15:22–29). Like other writers, Luke would have had to do research to get his information.

The material in Luke 1 and 2, so familiar to many Christians, is a good example of the kind of research Luke might have done. At the time Luke writes his Gospel, many persons mentioned in those two chapters had died. (Jesus is, of course, alive, having ascended into heaven.) Luke's source is probably Mary herself. She would have known what she and the angel Gabriel discussed and what Elizabeth said when Mary visited her, and she alone would have known what she was "pondering in her heart" when the shepherds came to the manger (Luke 2:19).

Although we cannot prove it, Luke could very well have interviewed Mary personally. If Luke wrote Luke and Acts during Paul's Roman imprisonment (AD 58–60), and if Mary gave birth to Jesus when she was in her early or middle teen years,[5] she would only have been in her early eighties at the time of the interview. Tradition locates her in her later years in Ephesus where the beloved disciple, John, conducted his ministry.[6] This would have been close enough to Rome for Luke to make the journey without seriously interrupting his time with Paul.[7]

In his introduction, Luke claims to write an orderly account. This commonly means a chronological or sequential account of Jesus' life and public ministry and of how the Gospel got from Jerusalem to Rome. However, it doesn't mean that Luke could have pulled together certain teachings of Jesus under a specific topic or that every detail of his account is exactly chronological, but it does mean that Luke writes an accurate and coherent history of Jesus (Gospel of Luke) and of the Gospel's spread (Book of Acts, which is clearly chronological in its accounts).

Inspiration is not like dictation, but a more personal and subtle guidance of the writer to set down exactly the words God has chosen. The writer uses all his faculties and abilities in the process.

We have shown how Luke's process may have included an interview with Mary. However, it also is possible that Luke received his information from other sources. That possibility in no way undermines the fact that Luke wrote an inspired, inerrant account.

Peter addresses the subject of inspiration in 2 Peter 1:16–21. He reminds his readers of the transfiguration, which he personally witnessed

(Matthew 17:1–2; Mark 9:2; Luke 9:28–36). There, God's words confirmed the glory of Jesus. So also, Peter argues, the words of the Old Testament writers come from God, not from man (2 Peter 1:21). Peter includes New Testament writings as part of Holy Scripture in 2 Peter 3:15–16, where he classes Paul's writings with "the other Scriptures."

The point, then, is this: Jesus, the Word of God (John 1:1–18), is both human and divine. The Holy Scriptures, the written Word of God, also have a divine side (origin, inspiration) and a human side (the authors and their world). Part of the adventure of Bible study is the investigation into the world of the authors of the books in the Bible. The things we learn equip us to understand more fully what we are reading.

The Purpose of Scripture

The primary purpose of Scripture is to introduce us to Jesus Christ as our Savior and Lord (John 20:30–31). Read 2 Timothy 3:10–17 and answer the following:

1. What does it mean to say that Scripture is "breathed out by God"?
2. Paul lists four functions of Scripture in verse 16. What are they?
3. What practical, day-to-day purpose does Scripture have?

"Breathed out by God" is a translation of *inspired.* This tells us that the source and essential characteristic of Scripture is that it comes from God and is God's own Word. Scripture does not merely *contain* the Word of God; it *is* the Word of God, as Jesus affirms in John 10:35 when He uses the two terms synonymously. The Bible is the source and standard for our teaching; it rebukes us (condemns us of our sin) and corrects us (guides us in the way that we should live). Confident of our salvation in Jesus Christ, we are thus completely equipped to live a life that honors God and shows others the way to salvation (see also Ephesians 2:8–10).[8]

Chapter 14 Notes

1. Scholars are divided on the dates of many of the New Testament books.
2. Connection to an apostle was not an absolute requirement for canonization, as is apparent from the fact that the Book of Hebrews was accepted as authoritative even though it has no clear connection with an apostle.

3. This does not mean that mistakes have not been made in copying the autographs or in translating the original languages. We shall discuss this further in the next section.
4. In Acts 16:10, Luke switches from the third person ("they") to the first person ("we"), indicating that he joined Paul, Silas, and Timothy on the second missionary journey (about AD 50).
5. An error in calculation by the monk who invented our system of counting years (Dionysius Exiguus) is responsible for the odd fact that Jesus was born in 2 BC (Before Christ), about a year before the death of Herod the Great.
6. Travelers to Ephesus today are often taken to the house that is said to have been Mary's house. Jesus had commended Mary into John's care at the cross (John 19:26).
7. Luke was a very faithful companion of Paul. At the end, shortly before Paul was executed, everyone had deserted him except Luke (2 Timothy 4:11).
8. For readers interested in learning more about a practical understanding of the doctrines of inspiration and inerrancy, consult William Arndt's *Bible Difficulties and Seeming Contradictions*, Robert G. Hoerber and Walter R. Roehrs, eds. (St. Louis: Concordia, 1987).

Chapter 15

English Translations and Paraphrases

ONE OF THE MOST IMPORTANT ACCOMPLISHMENTS OF MARTIN Luther, the sixteenth-century German reformer, was that he translated the Bible from the original languages into the common language of his day. By doing so, he empowered people to read the Bible for themselves. Only one English translation, the King James Version (KJV, produced in 1611) has come close to the popularity of Luther's German Bible. However, the KJV was not the first English translation.

John Wycliffe produced an English translation of the medieval Bible, the Latin Vulgate,[1] in the fourteenth century. Not long after that, the Medieval Church banned all translations. It became a capital crime to translate the Bible from its original Hebrew or Greek, or to translate the Latin Vulgate, into a modern language. This did not stop translation efforts. William Tyndale, the "Father of the English Bible," translated the New Testament and parts of the Old Testament before he was arrested and executed in 1536. A number of other English translations followed, but all were overshadowed by the translation ordered by King James, completed in 1611.

A team of fifty-four translators worked for seven years to produce what would become the most popular English Bible of all time. It underwent a number of revisions over the following decades, but remained largely the Bible that had been presented to King James.

The appearance of so many modern translations has confused people, particularly those who had come to love the KJV. When someone goes online or into a Christian bookstore to buy a Bible, the variety of choices can be intimidating. Some translations are better than others, so how do we pick the "right" one? Paraphrases differ from translations, but they are easier to read. Should we buy a paraphrase or a translation? And finally, why are there so many translations and paraphrases?

Common Bible Translations with Abbreviations

Contemporary English Version	CEV
English Standard Version	ESV
Good News Translation	GNT
Jerusalem Bible	JB
King James Version/New King James Version	KJV/NKJV
The Living Bible/New Living Translation	TLB/NLT
New American Bible, Revised Edition	NABRE
New American Standard Bible	NASB
New Century Version	NCV
New International Version	NIV
Revised English Bible	REB
Revised Standard Version/New Revised Standard Version	RSV/NRSV

Translation

The words in one language don't "line up" exactly with the words in another language. That is to say, every word has the possibility of communicating one or more meanings. The ranges of meanings a word can communicate are not identical from one language to the next.

As an example, let's look at the Greek word *pneuma.* We get our English words *pneumonia* and *pneumatic* from this word. Depending on context, *pneuma* can be accurately translated into English as *spirit*, or as *breath*, as *wind*, or even as a reference to the Holy Spirit. In the right context, it can refer to the whole self of a person (as in Mary's Magnificat, Luke 1:47).[2] No English word has the capacity to mean all these different things, so the translator must make many difficult choices.

Every translation reflects these choices. As a result, translations differ from one another. An additional problem occurs when English itself changes over a period of time. Take Psalm 7:9 as an example. In the last line of that verse, the King James reads, "For the righteous God trieth the hearts and reins."

The English language no longer uses *reins* in the way that the King James translators meant it. There, the word *reins* referred to the kidneys. Still, it is not much of an improvement to translate it "For the righteous God trieth the hearts and kidneys." The meaning of the psalmist doesn't become clear to us until we realize that *trieth* means "put to the test," that *heart* refers to the organ of thought and will (that is, the mind), and that kidneys were thought to be the seat of emotion (what we today would call the heart). Here, the English Standard Version has a better translation, "You who test the minds and hearts, O righteous God!"

The translator has to decide whether to stick as close as possible to vocabulary and word order (syntax) or to render the thought more freely, making the thought (rather than the words) clearer in the receptor language. That is to say, shall the translator give us a "literal" translation or a "dynamic" translation? Most translations try to stay as literal as possible, while most paraphrases are unabashedly dynamic. We can imagine a scale from 1 to 100 where "1" reflects the impossible perfect literal translation and "100" represents the freest possible paraphrase (which may have little actual connection to the original text). All translations fall somewhere on such a scale.

Rabbi Judah (second century AD) may have said it best when he stated that anyone claiming to make a literal translation is a liar and that someone who creates a paraphrase is a blasphemer and libeler (worthy of execution; see the Babylonian Talmud tractate *Kiddushin 49a*). Every translation reflects the philosophy, beliefs, and theological orientation of the translator. The best translations minimize this, but the background of the translator is always present.

As if all this were not enough, translators currently struggle with yet another issue: should the translation be gender-neutral, or should it reflect the gender bias of the original languages? For example, Paul uses the phrase "sons of God" in Romans 8:14, 19, and Galatians 3:26 to refer to all believers, men and women. Should the translator let stand the phrase "sons of God" or should it be changed to "children of God"? By extension, Jesus teaches us to pray to the "Father" (Matthew 6:9; Luke 11:2). Should this be changed to "parent"? Jesus would then become the "child" of the heavenly "parent" instead of Son of the Father. We can see how questions of translation often involve much larger questions of theology.

Current English Bibles

"Of making many books there is no end, and much study is a weariness of the flesh" (Ecclesiastes 12:12). What Solomon said about books in the tenth century BC is still true today, including different versions of the Bible. We won't discuss every translation available but will concentrate on five popular versions: King James/New King James Version, Revised Standard/New Revised Standard Version, New American Standard Bible, New International Version, and the English Standard Version.

The King James Version/New King James Version

As noted earlier, this translation goes back to the early seventeenth century. The richness of language, the beauty of its poetical sections, and the reliability and consistency of translation continue to make it an excellent choice for the modern Bible reader. Two weaknesses, however, should be noted.

The original language texts upon which the KJV was based were produced very late. Much earlier copies of the Hebrew and Greek manuscripts have been found since the KJV translators did their work. The three best-known New Testament examples are Mark 16:9–20 (the ending of Mark); John 7:53–8:11 (the story of the woman caught in the act of adultery); and 1 John 5:7–8 (technically known as the *Johannine Comma*). Ancient manuscripts discovered in the last century or so have indicated that these three sections were not part of the original writing (the autograph). A number of other, much smaller differences exist between the oldest and best manuscripts of the Bible and the Hebrew and Greek texts that the KJV translators had in their day

Secondly, the English language has changed somewhat since the KJV was prepared in 1611. For example, we no longer use the same second person pronouns or certain verb forms. ("Thou gavest me the book" is now "You gave me the book.") The second person singular forms of pronouns ("thou, thee, thine") have disappeared, replaced by the plural forms ("you, your"). Verb endings have disappeared (e.g., "-est"). Words have altered meaning as well. Instead of "suffer little children," we would say, "let the little children" (Matthew 19:14). Likewise, it makes little sense today to ask if the living will "prevent" the dead at the second coming of Jesus (1 Thessalonians 4:15). *Prevent*, from the Latin *pre venio* ("I come before"), denoted an advantage. Will the living precede the dead at the resurrection? That is, will the living have an advantage over the dead when Jesus returns? Paul answers no, but modern readers of the KJV might have a hard time understanding the question.

The New King James Version, introduced in 1982, offers a new translation of the Greek and Hebrew originals along the lines of the KJV but without the peculiarities (anachronisms) of the seventeenth century. Its biggest weakness is that, like the KJV, it does not take into account recent manuscript discoveries.

The Revised Standard Version/New Revised Standard Version

The Revised Standard Version first appeared as a New Testament (1946) and then with the Old Testament (1952). It was a new translation from the Hebrew and Greek and took into account the manuscript discoveries up to that point.

The theological orientation of the translators may be seen in places where word choice or punctuation is critical. For example, in Isaiah 7:14 the prophet predicts that a virgin will give birth to a child whose name will be Immanuel. Matthew believes this is fulfilled when Mary, a virgin, gives birth to Jesus (Matthew 1:23). The Hebrew word translated *virgin* in the KJV is translated *young woman* in the RSV. In making this choice, was the RSV committee reluctant to support the traditional understanding that this passage refers to the virgin birth of Jesus? Their choice in this case raised great concern.

Some have criticized the RSV punctuation in Romans 9:5. The original manuscripts contained no punctuation. Editors and translators determined where to place the punctuation marks. The RSV reads, "To them belong the patriarchs, and of their race, according to the flesh, is the Christ. God who is over all be blessed for ever. Amen." The period after *Christ* avoided calling Jesus *God* in this verse, raising further concern that the translators were sometimes hesitant to reflect fully the teachings of the Bible or how Christians understood them from the earliest days of the Church.

The New Revised Standard Version (1989) has changed this, altering the period to a comma, so that it now reads, "To them belong the patriarchs, and from them, according to the flesh, comes the Messiah, who is over all, God blessed forever. Amen." The NRSV revision allows Paul to identify Jesus as God at this point. The NRSV has gained respect and acceptance, although some criticize it for using gender-neutral terminology ("inclusive language") in many places.

The New American Standard Bible

The New American Standard Bible (NASB) became available in 1971. It is a conservative translation that tries to maintain the original verb tenses (and other elements of speech) in its translation. The NASB lends itself very well to Bible study. However, when read aloud, it often sounds a bit wooden. It was updated in 1995 and is more fluid than its predecessor, conforming more to American syntax and grammar.

The New International Version

Published first in 1978, the New International Version (NIV) has been somewhat of a standard in many churches and homes for several years. It is much easier to read aloud and is reasonably conservative as a translation. The NIV underwent minor revisions in 1984, and a more thorough rework in 2011 has caused some church bodies to evaluate this translation less favorably. In an effort to make the translation easier to read, scholars moved away from a word-for-word approach to a more "dynamic equivalent" philosophy. Additional concern has been voiced over its move toward gender-inclusive language in the 2011 version. As noted above, every translation reflects the faith system of the translators, and the NIV is no exception (evangelical Protestant). As with all translations, it could be improved at places.[3]

The English Standard Version

The ESV traces its family tree back to the work of William Tyndale (1526) and the King James Version (1611). The Revised Standard Version (1971 edition) in particular serves as the launch point for the English Standard Version. If it can be said that the NIV has been slowly moving from the literal translation side of our 1–100 scale toward the paraphrase end, the ESV seeks to reestablish an "essentially literal" translation much closer to the 1 end of that scale. First published in 2001 and recently revised in 2011, the ESV strives to keep a word-for-word approach and, where possible, retain gender-specific language ("man" rather than "person" or "human being" where the original text has "man" used inclusively of both men and women). The essentially literal approach is designed to minimize the impact of the translator on the translation, giving the reader as much access as possible to the text in all of its complexity and with all of its challenges.

Paraphrases

A paraphrase is a very dynamic rendering of the Bible intended to make the meaning more evident. Sometimes the paraphrase starts by using the Greek and Hebrew, and sometimes not.

The Good News Translation

The Good News Translation (GNT), which was first published in 1976 as the Good News Bible or Today's English Version, is a very popular paraphrase. It was produced by the American Bible Society with the intent that it would be readable by the vast majority of English speakers. Language was to be kept "natural, clear, simple, and unambiguous."

Perhaps the biggest weakness of the GNT is that it tends to make the rich language of Scripture so simple as to sound flat. For example, Jesus uses the word *blessed* in the Beatitudes (Matthew 5:1–12). The GNT renders that word as *happy.* "Happy are those who are humble" (v. 5) does not convey the point Jesus makes: the meek (as the ESV translates it) here are blessed because in the future they will inherit the kingdom of God, the new heaven and new earth, which follows the resurrection. Jesus promises more to the meek than the happiness usually associated with the word *happy* today. He says that those who do not insist upon their own way but put faith in Jesus Christ will find themselves inheriting the world. Some who follow Jesus' directions will end up like He did, without even a place to lay their heads (Matthew 8:20). God's gracious favor (blessedness) on the believer reaches its culmination in the next age. The GNT's *happy* can turn the rich and complex *blessed* into the flat and misleading *happy*.

Contemporary English Version

In 1995, the American Bible Society published the Contemporary English Version (CEV) in an effort to make the Bible more accessible to people around the world due to its lower reading level. In this translation, the beatitude about the meek (Matthew 5:5) reads, "God blesses those people who are humble. The earth will belong to them!" Like the NRSV, the CEV uses gender-neutral terminology in many places.

The Living Bible

Kenneth Taylor's The Living Bible (TLB, 1971) has become very popular. It is a retelling of the biblical story based on the American Standard Version, with the goal that it be simple and understandable. It is indeed simple and understandable, but it often departs greatly from the biblical text. Two examples will illustrate the point.

In 1 Corinthians 16:24, Paul writes, "My love *be* with you all in Christ Jesus. Amen." This is a fairly literal translation (from the ESV). It supplies the verb *be*, since the original does not explicitly state the verb.[4] The Living Bible reads, "My love to all of you, for we all belong to Christ Jesus. Sincerely, Paul." The Living Bible rendition is easy to read and understand, but it is not what God inspired Paul to write.

A more significant variation occurs at Revelation 13:18. In this famous "666" passage, two beasts, one from the sea and one from the land, appear to help Satan fight Christians. The first beast (13:1–10) represents anti-Christian government. The second beast (13:11–18) represents anti-Christian religion. Both are symbols of patterns that will occur throughout the New Testament age. Faced with governmental persecution, the Christian needs endurance and faith (13:10b). Faced with deceptive religions, the Christian needs wisdom from God (13:18). A fairly literal translation of 13:18 reads, "Here is *the need for* wisdom. The one having a mind, let him calculate the number of the beast, for it is man's number, and his number is 666."

Two big questions present themselves. What does the number 666 represent, and does it refer to one man or to more than one man? Strictly speaking, one can translate *man's* as "a man's," although this is very unlikely. Had John meant one specific man, he could have said "a certain man" or "one man." It is far more likely that John intends us to understand that 666 (a symbolic number that refers to man's failed efforts to become God) applies to the whole human race and specifically to false teachers.[5]

Alternative ways of interpreting 666 include *gematria* (counting the numerical value of the letters in a name) and *triangulation* of numerical relationships (1 through 8 added together = 36, 1 through 36 added together = 666, therefore the important number is 8, which makes the 36 and the 666 possible. Eight would then be given symbolic value). A good translation or paraphrase will translate this verse in such a way as to let you, the reader, make the interpretation. A bad translation will take all options away from the reader, leaving you with only the translator's opinion. Some translations render "number of a person" (NRSV), and others "number of a man" (NKJV, NIV, ESV). The best translation lets the English reader wrestle with the text. TLB takes all choice away and misleads the reader with Kenneth Taylor's own millennialist theology and belief that "666" is an example of *gematria*: "Here is a puzzle that calls for careful thought to solve it. Let those who are able, interpret this code: the numerical values of the letters in his name add to 666!" (TLB).

Paraphrases in general, and The Living Bible in particular, are best when you want to read long sections of the Bible in a short time. They tend not to be very good for verse-by-verse Bible study, because so much of the translator's opinion is included in the transmission process from the original language text to the English. They also hide the meanings of individual words and of phrases in the Bible as they echo one another and build on one another's thoughts. These are features of the Bible best realized with a literal translation. A recent revision of this paraphrase, now called the New Living Translation (NLT), attempts to address the weaknesses of the original TLB.

Choosing the Right Bible

Perhaps the place to start is to ask the question, "What do I want to do with my Bible?" If I want to read the entire Bible in twelve months, perhaps a good paraphrase is best. If I need to prepare a Sunday School lesson, then maybe I should buy a study Bible. If you do buy a study Bible, remember that the notes are not God's Word—only the text itself is.

You may also want to ask a friend or someone at church who teaches Bible classes what they would recommend. A well-informed clerk at a Christian bookstore also could help you. Don't be afraid to look through several editions to see which one offers you the extras that you want.

When examining a Bible, check passages that reveal the translators' orientation. We have already noted Isaiah 7:14; Matthew 5:5; Romans 9:5; and Revelation 13:18. Also take time to read the introduction. Those pages that precede Genesis 1 might tell you all you need to learn about a particular Bible. Last, but certainly not least, pray about your choice. Also pray each time you start your Bible study. Ask the Holy Spirit to guide you. Why not also ask Him to help you choose the best one for you? After all, who knows a book better than its author?

Chapter 15 Notes

1. In the fourth century AD, Jerome translated the Hebrew and Greek manuscripts into Latin, the common language ("vulgar tongue") of his day. The Roman Catholic Church adopted this as its official Bible.

2. Hebrew has no reflexive pronoun. You cannot say "myself" in Hebrew. Instead, you would say "my soul" or "my spirit." Mary's use of "spirit" in the Magnificat reflects this Hebrew idiom.
3. Certainly the title for God could be improved. The NIV renders *Adonai Yahweh* as "Sovereign LORD" (e.g., Genesis 15:2). Perhaps the names of God could simply be transliterated (as above) with an introductory note on their meaning.
4. This is quite common in Greek texts and is called "ellipsis." The reader is expected to fill in the verb.
5. This is confirmed by practical experience. Many religious teachers, especially in the New Age movement, proclaim that we are "gods."

Chapter 16

Ancient Books and Writings Outside the Bible

DOES THE BIBLE CONTAIN ALL THE BOOKS WRITTEN DURING ancient times? Certainly not! Only a few of the works produced by ancient authors appear in the Bible. In fact, a number of epistles and gospels claimed to have been written by apostles were never considered Scripture. Not even all the letters written by New Testament authors were preserved. We have evidence for at least three letters of Paul that have not survived.[1] The modern Bible student may well ask what kinds of literature existed during Bible times, and what impact, if any, does that literature have on Bible study?

In this section, we will look at three groups of books: the Dead Sea Scrolls, Old Testament Apocrypha and Pseudepigrapha, and the Nag Hammadi Library.

The Dead Sea Scrolls

Of all the literature outside of the Bible in ancient times, the Dead Sea Scrolls are probably now the most well known. In 1947, an Arab youth, a shepherd looking for his goats, accidentally discovered some ancient manuscripts preserved in sealed jars and hidden in a cave near the Dead Sea. Over the next ten years, archaeologists found a number of additional manuscripts in other caves. Eleven relatively complete scrolls were eventually discovered, along with thousands of fragments of other scrolls, some as small as a fingernail.

The scrolls and scroll fragments fall into three categories: books of the Old Testament,[2] commentaries on the Old Testament,[3] and sectarian writings.[4] These were apparently preserved by a group of religious separatists who were eradicated by the Romans in AD 70. Josephus, an ancient historian, mentions a group of separatists living in this area. He called them Essenes. Many scholars think the Dead Sea Scrolls belonged to these people.

The most immediate and obvious benefit from these scrolls is that we have verified the reliability of the Hebrew Scriptures. About 95 percent of the Bible texts at Qumran (the name for the place where the scrolls were found) conform to the type of Hebrew text preserved in the Masoretic text as it was passed down to us.[5]

These scrolls, especially the documents originating with the Essene sect, made a second contribution. They provide a window into one of the many diverse groups that made up Judaism in the first century AD. We see a group of people who, like John the Baptist, rejected the more mainstream Judaism of the Pharisees and Sadducees. In fact, shortly after the discovery of the Dead Sea Scrolls some people thought John the Baptist might have spent some time in the Qumran community, but those suggestions have largely fallen out of favor among scholars. The people who lived at Qumran believed themselves to be the true Israel. They looked for the arrival of the messianic age and the destruction of their enemies in Jerusalem. The Romans, however, destroyed the Qumran village.

Have the Dead Sea Scrolls changed the Bible at all? Not really. In a few places, modern translations of the Old Testament (especially the NRSV) have taken into account the Hebrew Scriptures found at Qumran. Aside from a few small alterations in the Old Testament, the Dead Sea Scrolls have not challenged the text of the Bible. These small alterations have not changed any doctrines. They have been most important for helping us understand the history of Old Testament manuscripts and the Jewish people who valued them.

One can find many inexpensive books on the Dead Sea Scrolls. These three provide a sample:

Geza Vermes. *The Complete Dead Sea Scrolls in English.* London: Penguin Books, 2012.

Hershel Shanks, ed. *Understanding the Dead Sea Scrolls: A Reader from the Biblical Archaeology Review.* New York: Random House, 1992.

Hershel Shanks, James C. VanderKam, P. Kyle McCarter Jr., and James A. Sanders. *The Dead Sea Scrolls After Forty Years.* Washington DC: Biblical Archaeology Society, 1992.

Old Testament Apocrypha and Pseudepigrapha

We also need to distinguish between those books that are considered part of Scripture and those that are nonbiblical. If you look at a Roman Catholic Bible, you will see that it has several more books in the Old Testament than does a typical Protestant Bible. These books are Tobit, Judith, Additions to the Book of Esther, Wisdom of Solomon, Ecclesiasticus (also known as the Wisdom of Jesus Son of Sirach), Baruch, the Letter of Jeremiah (or Baruch 6), Additions to the Book of Daniel (the Prayer of Azariah and the Son of the Three Young Men, Susanna, Bel and the Dragon), and 1 and 2 Maccabees. They are available in a new study edition using the ESV, *The Apocrypha: The Lutheran Edition with Notes* (Concordia, 2012; a study guide is also available). Another good edition is the *New Oxford Annotated Apocrypha*, fourth edition (Oxford, 2010).

The Roman Catholic, Greek Orthodox, and Russian Orthodox churches accept these books as authoritative. Most Protestants do not regard these as canonical, because they were never part of the Hebrew Scriptures. However, the Greek translation of the Old Testament (the Septuagint) contained these books. Since Jerome included these books in his Latin Vulgate, and since the Vulgate is the official Bible of the Roman Catholic Church, they were considered Scripture. Protestants called these works *apocryphal*, but the Roman Catholic Church designates them as *deuterocanonical* ("secondary canon"). They are worth reading—particularly 1 and 2 Maccabees, which trace the history of the Jewish people in the first and second centuries before Christ.

A second category of books is designated as *Pseudepigrapha* (Greek "false signatures"). These writings were produced throughout the intertestamental period (about 400 BC to the birth of Christ) and into the New Testament age. The books claim to be written by famous people of the past (e.g., Moses, Enoch, the Twelve Patriarchs). James Charlesworth has collected fifty-two writings that have these five elements in common:

1. The writings have a Jewish or Christian origin.[6]

2. They are attributed to the great figures of Jewish history.
3. They claim to be a communication from God.
4. They reflect Old Testament narratives.
5. They were composed sometime between 200 BC and AD 200.

Some of these books are simpler storytelling (e.g., the Testament of the Twelve Patriarchs), while others are more apocalyptic like Revelation (1 Enoch). Some "fill in the gaps" in the Old Testament, adding stories about minor characters (like Jannes and Jambres, the two magicians who battled Moses in Pharaoh's court). Others reflect more current history (like the Letter of Aristeas, which tells how the Septuagint [the Greek translation of the Hebrew Scriptures] was made).

How do these works help us study the Bible? First, they give us added insight into the world in which Jesus conducted His earthly ministry. As a result of reading some of these books, we can better appreciate the diversity of thought and the differences between the divisions within first-century Judaism.

Second, we get a clearer picture of the messianic expectations people held at the time of Christ. For example, in the Psalms of Solomon (written in the first century BC), we read of the coming Messiah and the destruction that He will bring to Gentiles and to sinners in general (Psalms of Solomon 17:21–25). This work reveals the expectation that when the Messiah came, He would set up a glorious kingdom of wealth and power, like His ancestor David.

Some of the apostles may have had this in mind when they left their homes, families, and careers to follow Jesus. They expected a really big payday when Jesus established an earthly kingdom. This is obvious from the times the disciples argued among themselves as to who was the greatest. The request of James and John to sit on Jesus' right and left in His glorious kingdom (Mark 10:35–37) indicates that they looked for an earthly kingdom. Perhaps Peter speaks for the entire band when he asks Jesus what payment they will receive for following Jesus (Matthew 19:27). They expected to receive this payment once Jesus set up the kind of kingdom anticipated in many of the Pseudepigrapha.

The Nag Hammadi Library

Like the Dead Sea Scrolls, the Nag Hammadi Library was an accidental discovery. Stored in a clay jar,[7] thirteen documents from as early as the third and fourth centuries AD were discovered in Egypt. Their discovery turned out to be much more dramatic than that of the Dead Sea Scrolls, involving intrigue, theft, murder, and even cannibalism.[8]

Writers from heretical Christian sects apparently wrote the Nag Hammadi documents. The writings reflect a type of false teaching broadly known as *Gnosticism*. Gnosticism generally emphasized secret knowledge, denied the bodily existence (incarnation) of Christ as well as the crucifixion, and had a strong interest in angels. (Ancient Gnosticism and the modern New Age philosophy have much in common—particularly cosmic dualism, angelology, a rejection of the cross of Christ, and a habit of adopting beliefs from other religions and philosophies.) The best known of these works is the Gospel of Thomas. At the end of this collection of supposed sayings of Jesus, we read,

> Simon Peter said to them: Let Mary go away from us, for women are not worthy of life. Jesus said: Lo, I shall lead her, so that I may make her a male, and that she too may become a living spirit (*pneuma*), resembling you males. For every woman who makes herself a male will enter the kingdom of heaven.[9]

We easily recognize that this teaching stands in opposition to the clear teaching of the Bible. Holy Scripture teaches that women are created in the image of God (Genesis 1:26–27), are equally part of God's family of believers (Galatians 3:26–29), and are fellow heirs of the kingdom of God (1 Peter 3:7).

Does the Nag Hammadi Library affect our faith? No, it has no impact on the Bible or on our Christian beliefs. It does show us that early Christianity faced challenges other than persecution and the pressure of pagan religions. Christians also had to fight against heretical movements that claimed Jesus as their founder too.

The Nag Hammadi Library contains a number of other works that are produced under the title "gospel" or under the name of an apostle. Although these writings are interesting, they don't really have any direct relationship to the New Testament. The following books provide additional information about the Nag Hammadi Library:

Charles W. Hedrick and Robert Hodgson, Jr. *Nag Hammadi, Gnosticism, and Early Christianity*. Peabody: Hendrickson Publishers, 1986.

Elaine Pagels. *The Gnostic Gospels*. New York: Random House, 1989.

John McRay. *Archaeology and the New Testament*. Grand Rapids: Baker Academic, 2008.

Wilhelm Schneemelcher, ed. *New Testament Apocrypha*. 2 vols. Cambridge: James Clarke & Co., 1991.

Willis Barnstone, ed. *The Other Bible*. San Francisco: HarperOne, 2005.

Summary and Conclusions

The Dead Sea Scrolls and other extra-canonical books do not challenge our confidence in the Holy Scriptures. They provide background information that helps us study the Bible with understanding as we learn more about the ancient world. By reading these books, we may even appreciate the Bible more than before!

Scripture is straightforward, honest about our sin, and crystal clear about our Savior, Jesus Christ. The adventure of Bible study begins anew each day. Along the way, we may take time to pick up some history or read books that people wrote during the same centuries the Bible was being written. We come to know God's Word better as we grow in our ability to understand what He says and apply it to our lives. May God bless you as you continue to read the Word, pray for the Spirit's guidance, and share it with others!

Chapter 16 Notes

1. Paul refers to a previous letter to the Corinthians, now lost, in 1 Corinthians 5:9–13. He mentions a "severe letter" to Corinth, written between 1 and 2 Corinthians, in 2 Corinthians 2:3–9 and 7:8–12. That letter has not been found. Paul also commends to the Colossians the letter he wrote to the Laodiceans, but we do not have such a letter today.
2. About one fourth of the texts are biblical texts, representing every book of the Old Testament except Esther. It may be significant that Esther is the only Hebrew Scripture that does not mention God.
3. These include commentaries as well as meditations on the Bible, such as hymns and psalms.
4. Some of these are religious, some are not. One of them, the Copper Scroll, seems to be a treasure map!

5. The Hebrew text that was formerly the oldest copy of the Old Testament is known as the "Leningrad Codex" (a codex is a type of book) dating to approximately AD 1000.
6. In *The Old Testament Pseudepigrapha* (Garden City, NY: Doubleday, 1985), James Charlesworth notes that the lone exception is Ahiqar.
7. Jeremiah also stored important documents in a clay jar in the sixth century BC (Jeremiah 32:14).
8. Both McRay's book and Pagels's volume tell the story of their discovery.
9. Logion 118, taken from *Synopsis Quattuor Evangeliorum* (Stuttgart: Württembergische Bibelanstalt, 1964), page 530.

Part Four

Putting It All to Work

In the first three parts of the book, you learned key principles for interpreting the Bible, how to interpret various types of literature in the Bible, how we got our Bible, and resources that enrich our understanding of it. Part four will prepare you to explore the Bible more completely, overcome challenges, and share with others what you have learned.

Chapter 17

Sensitive to a Different Culture: "The Friend at Midnight" (Luke 11:5-8)

HAVING EXPLORED MANY DIFFERENT ASPECTS OF BIBLE STUDY, we may now put all these tools into practice. For this purpose, the parable of the friend at midnight will serve as a helpful example. The broader context of Scripture, the writing of Luke, and the immediate context of Luke 11:1–13 form the background for reading this parable. At the same time, without a sensitivity to the cultural context of the original audience, the modern translator (and reader) easily misses the point of Jesus' story. Reading and understanding this parable requires us to use a number of the principles we have discussed as well as several of the resources we have mentioned.

This parable answers the question "Why should God answer my prayers?" If God's response depends on me, then prayer is a "Law thing" that we do to get what we want from God. If God's response depends on His love and promise in Christ Jesus, then prayer is a "Gospel thing." He decides what we get and when.

We first spend a few moments in prayer, asking the Holy Spirit's guidance and blessing as we read. We then look at the section (Luke 11:1–13) in a variety of translations and paraphrases. If we don't have books available, excellent resources can be accessed on the Internet (such as BibleGateway.com).

We might first notice that Luke has a different account of the Lord's Prayer (compare Matthew 6:9–13). He has omitted the two references to heaven and the final petition about delivering us from evil/the evil one. Since Matthew wrote with a Jewish audience in mind, he could be confident they would understand heaven and know about the evil one. ("Evil" and "evil one" are both possible translations of the original Greek in Matthew 6:13.) Luke wrote for a Gentile audience who might have been confused about both these topics. In the interest of streamlining and simplifying, he may have then edited out the confusing material. (Material that Luke shares with Matthew and Mark is often shorter and simpler than either of those in the other Gospels.)

We might also remember that hospitality is an important duty in the culture of the Middle East (recall Abraham and the three visitors, Genesis 18:1–8). Western cultures don't generally place such a high value on hospitality nor do most people in the West consider it a failure of duty to offer little or no hospitality. It's important to remember that the Bible comes from the Middle East and reflects Eastern, not Western, culture and values. We could check a Bible handbook or a Bible dictionary to learn something about hospitality in that society (as in *Concordia's Complete Bible Handbook* [Concordia, 2013], p. 386). A quick Internet search on the subject will generate a number of websites that discuss the duty of hospitality, both for hosts as well as for guests, in this part of the world. We don't have such a strong sense of obligation toward visitors in our culture, so we should be alert to clues in the text that will give us direction for interpreting this parable.

We have already noted that patterns of usage can help us understand a particularly challenging text. In the parable of the friend at midnight, a quick concordance search for "Which of you . . ." reveals an important clue to the parable: Jesus paints a picture that is theoretically possible but highly unlikely to happen in the real world (such as Luke 11:11–12; 12:25; 14:28). When Jesus asks, "Which of you," the answer He expects is "no one." In other words, when our Lord opens with this phrase, He expects His listeners (and readers) to understand that people will never actually do what He's talking about (like giving a snake to your son when he asks for food!).

At this point, we may recognize that we need a little help with the parable, perhaps from a good commentary. Eventually, we may turn up the work of Dr. Kenneth Bailey, a man who lived and taught in the Mideast for forty years. He has written extensively on the parables of Luke and offers an invaluable insight into the parable of the friend at midnight" (*Poet & Peasant And Through Peasant Eyes* [Eerdmans, 1983], pp. 119–41). He argues that the word translated "impudence" (ESV), "importunity" (KJV), and "shameless audacity" (NIV) should be translated "shamelessness" (a literal rendering of the Greek original). It refers in that culture to a positive virtue of "avoiding shame or failure." In Luke 11:8, it describes the man inside the house, not the man outside the house. If Dr. Bailey is right, then the man inside the house gets up and responds to his neighbor's request because the man inside the house fulfills the Middle Eastern duty of hospitality. The qualities of integrity and honor ("righteousness" as "fulfills his obligation") move the inside man to act.

This would mean that God answers prayer because He is righteous, He does not fail or shame Himself by not keeping His Word (see Psalm 50:15). Prayer becomes a "Gospel thing" dependent on God's character and promise and not a "Law thing" dependent on our performance or persistence. (For a parable on constancy in prayer, see Luke 18:1–8.)

Does the context support this understanding?

First, the inside man gives the outside man far more than is asked. The outside man wanted to set a full meal before his surprise visitor (like Abraham in Genesis 18) and was going to ask a number of his neighbors to help. This avoided burdening any one neighbor with giving enough food for a whole meal. In this parable, the outside man asks only for three loaves of bread, just the beginning of the meal. Yet the inside man gives the outside man as much as the outside man needs for the whole meal. This is not the act of a man irritated at being disturbed in the middle of the night! The inside man reveals the extent of his righteousness and generosity by giving the outside man far more than is requested, everything that he needs.

Second, Luke adds three short statements (Luke 11:9–10) to confirm the point of the parable (that prayer is a "Gospel thing" dependent on God's character and not on our performance). Everyone who asks, receives, everyone who seeks, finds. To everyone who knocks, the door opens. That's a 100 percent success rate. If prayer is a "Law thing" dependent on our persistence, impudence, and performance, what are the odds that 100 percent will succeed? Only if prayer is a "Gospel thing," dependent on God and His grace, is 100 percent possible.

Third, Jesus points out that even evil people know how to give good gifts to their children (Luke 11:11–13). The contrast here is not between those children who persist asking and those who give up, but between human beings (who are evil) and God (who is good). God answers our prayers because He has promised to do so for all His children through faith in His Son, Jesus Christ (for example, John 14:13–14). Our Father will give us far more than we ask—He will give us His Holy Spirit (Luke 11:13; John 14:16).

Conclusion

In this reading of the parable of the friend at midnight, we have seen how to use a variety of principles (Scripture interprets Scripture, proper distinction between Law and Gospel, literary and cultural context, rule of faith) and a number of Bible study tools (concordance, Bible handbook, commentary, the Internet). We thank the Lord for so many resources and tools as we open His Word and seek to grow in our faith and discipleship. What a tremendous joy it is to know that our prayers are heard by our Father. As Luther explains the introduction to the Lord's Prayer, "Our Father who art in heaven," in his Small Catechism:

> With these words God tenderly invites us to believe that He is our true Father and that we are His true children, so that with all boldness and confidence we may ask Him as dear children ask their dear father.

Chapter 18

So You're Going to Teach a Bible Study

EACH BOOK OF THE BIBLE HAS A ROLE TO PLAY IN THE DRAMATIC story of Scripture. Like a mechanic looking at the parts of an internal combustion engine, the reader or Bible class leader needs to know how each part works within the whole and what job it does.

Each of the biblical books also has a structure of its own, an organization designed to communicate its message to the reader or hearer of the proclaimed Word. Inspired by the Holy Spirit, the author(s) selected each part and included its particular details intentionally. The modern reader of Scripture should ask why the author placed his material in the order we have it and how any one part connects to the material before and after it. Look for patterns of usage and be aware of the literary structures of the book. Read and reread the text. Slow down as much as possible.

People sometimes find themselves in challenging or new situations. Maybe a Sunday School teacher or Christian Day School teacher is invited to lead a class on one of the biblical books. Perhaps a member of a regular Bible study group has been given the task to lead the reading and discussion for a book or a section of Scripture. What to do?

Take it to the Lord in prayer. Talk to the Author of the Bible about this opportunity and responsibility to read His Word more closely. Ask the Holy Spirit to open your eyes and turn on the light of your mind as you read His Word. Pray to Jesus for wisdom as you prepare to lead His people in growth of faith and discipleship.

Read the whole book or section of Scripture. Try to read as much as possible in one sitting, seeing the "grand vista" (the big picture). Consider the book/section's place in the context of the Bible as a whole. If the Bible can be described as God's story, how does the book you are studying fit within the history of His interaction with human beings? What purpose does it serve? The following may serve as examples of how to get started in preparing a study.

Example 1: Deuteronomy (Law of Moses)

The Book of Deuteronomy prepares God's people for their entrance into the Promised Land (*Deuteronomy* means "second law" and refers to the repetition of the Ten Commandments in Deuteronomy 5). Following forty years in the wilderness, the new generation needed to be reminded of the covenant God had established with them on Mount Sinai (Exodus 19). The older generation passed away, as God had promised (see Numbers 14, especially vv. 29–30). Moses speaks both Law and Gospel to the younger generation as they contemplate their life in this land "flowing with milk and honey" (Exodus 3:8; Deuteronomy 6:3).

We can see the purpose of Deuteronomy reflected in the similarities and differences between the two sets of commandments (see the first set in Exodus 20). They seem identical except for the third commandment (or fourth, depending on how you number them). In Exodus 20:8–11, the Lord tells the people to set aside the Sabbath day (from Friday sundown to Saturday sundown) as holy (separate, special) and rest from the work they do the other six days of the week. The reason? God worked six days and rested on the seventh (Genesis 2:2–3). However, when Moses communicates the same commandments almost forty years later (1406 BC), the reason for observing the Sabbath or "Rest Day" has changed. The Sabbath finds its fulfillment as the people of God remember (reexperience, reconnect to; Deuteronomy 5:12–15) the exodus. The people will face terrible temptations in the Promised Land. They will be enticed to leave the one true God and pursue false gods (see Deuteronomy 8). By reconnecting to the great saving event of the exodus, they will remain connected to the God who saved them. The generation that Moses led out of Egypt would have had firsthand experience with this great event. Later generations could easily forget it. The Sabbath Day would serve as a weekly reminder of what the Lord had done for them. (We come together around Word and Sacrament for essentially the same reason today.)

Deuteronomy functions as the people's blueprint for surviving in the real world of Canaan with their faith and identity intact. By seeing the whole Book of Deuteronomy in this light, the book will seem less like a series of arbitrary rules and more like the unified, cohesive "contract" between God and His people that it really is. As Bible study leader, **remind the participants of Deuteronomy's purpose and goal**. As you read together the various passages of the book, help the group see how each of the parts fit into the whole.

Example 2: John (Gospel)

After answering the question: "How does this book fit into the whole of Scripture?" we turn to a second matter: **How do the parts of this book work together to achieve its purpose?** John states his purpose clearly in 20:31, "These are written so that you may believe that Jesus is the Christ, the Son of God, and that by believing you may have life in His name." Either by careful observation or by looking at the introduction to John in a good study Bible, you will notice that John divided his Gospel into two parts (the ministry of Jesus, beginning with 1:19, and the week of the Passion, beginning with the triumphal entry in 12:12). He also included an introduction (1:1–18) and an epilogue (ch. 21; remember that chapters and verses were added long after the Bible had been written).

John's introduction (1:1–18) differs from the birth narratives of Matthew (1:18–25) and Luke (2:1–21); Mark does not include a story about Jesus' birth). The introduction wastes no time in revealing Jesus as true God, creator of the world (1:1–4), incarnate light of salvation (1:9–14), and only-begotten God, who reveals the Father (1:17–18).

Just as John echoed the creation account in Genesis 1 in the first verse of his introduction ("In the beginning . . ."), so he built a seven-day highway leading to the first of seven signs (miracles) that point us to Jesus as God Incarnate, Savior of the world.[1] Jesus performs the first sign at a wedding in Cana, changing water into wine.[2] The result? "His disciples believed in Him" (John 2:11). John records the second sign in 4:46–54. Like the first, it takes place in Cana. Jesus heals the son of a local official without even laying hands on the child. He simply says to the distraught father, "Go; your son will live" (v. 50). The result? As with the first sign, it is faith. John writes of the father: "And he himself believed, and all his household" (v. 53). A pattern begins to emerge, consistent with the purpose of the Gospel (20:31). People see what Jesus does, and they put their faith in Him. So what happens in the third sign?

In John 5:1–15, Jesus heals a man at the Pool of Bethesda in the temple compound at Jerusalem at one of the three major Jewish festivals. As you prepare to lead participants in the reading of this section, ask them to note the details:

- It took place in the temple compound.
- It took place on the Sabbath (from Friday sundown to Saturday sundown).
- It took place by a pool (the Pool of Bethesda).
- The man had been an invalid for a long time, almost forty years.
- The man was interrogated by the Jewish religious authorities.

After the first and second signs, John commented on the faith of those who witnessed the sign (the disciples, the local official, and his household). He mentions no such response to this sign. In fact, Jesus confronts the man in the temple and says: "See, you are well! Sin no more,[3] that nothing worse may happen to you" (John 5:14). The man responds by going to the Jewish religious authorities and informing them that Jesus was the culprit who healed him on the Sabbath and told him to take up his mat and walk, in violation of their understanding of Sabbath laws.[4] The man shows no evidence of faith whatsoever. Rather, his actions reveal the sin of unbelief.

John records the fourth sign (feeding the five thousand) and the fifth sign (Jesus walks on white-capped water) in 6:1–21. In both signs, He reveals His divinity. As God had provided manna and quail in the wilderness (Exodus 16; Numbers 11), so Jesus provides bread and fish in the desolate region near the Sea of Galilee (see Matthew 14:13). As the Lord commanded the sea and the wind (as in the crossing of the Red Sea, Exodus 14), so nature itself submits to Jesus, its Creator and Lord.[5]

In the sixth sign, Jesus heals a man born blind (John 9). Note the parallels this sign shares with the third sign in John 5:

- It likely took place near the temple compound.
- It took place on the Sabbath (from Friday sundown to Saturday sundown).

- It involved a pool (the Pool of Siloam).
- The man had been an invalid for a long time, since birth.
- The man was interrogated by the Jewish religious authorities.

The results, however, are very different. Instead of reporting Jesus to the authorities to avoid possible punishment, this man confesses Jesus boldly. Cast out from the synagogue (9:34), the man born blind sees his Savior clearly. John 9:38 tells us, "He said, 'Lord, I believe,' and he worshiped Him."

Just as the first two signs shared a location (Cana in Galilee), so the third and sixth signs share a location (the temple in Jerusalem). Just as the fourth and fifth signs reflect Jesus' power over nature (multiplying bread and fish, walking on storm-tossed waves), so also the third and sixth signs reveal Jesus' power over incurable disabilities. Unlike the man in the third sign, the man in the sixth sign also comes to faith and worships his Savior. (Remember John's stated purpose in 20:31.)

John wove six signs together in chapters 2–9 of his Gospel in order to bring the reader to the seventh and final, climactic sign: the raising of Lazarus (John 11). A friend of Jesus named Lazarus falls ill. Lazarus's sisters, Mary and Martha, send for Jesus. Jesus intentionally delays His trip to Bethany, stating, "This illness does not lead to death. It is for the glory of God, so that the Son of God may be glorified through it" (11:4). As class leader, remind the participants of the disciples' question and Jesus' answer in John 9:1–5. The work of God is salvation through Jesus Christ, apparent in all the signs recorded by John.

With Lazarus dead for four days and buried,[6] Jesus arrives at Bethany. Martha first, then Mary, leaves the family and friends who have come to mourn with them to meet Jesus.[7] After speaking with each of them and offering a prayer (for the sake of the onlookers), Jesus calls Lazarus out of the tomb. He comes. The result? The Jewish leadership decides they have to kill Lazarus as well as Jesus "because on account of him many of the Jews were going away and believing in Jesus" (John 12:11).

As session leader, spend time with the details in chapter 11. John vividly portrays the humanity of Jesus (who sheds a tear of heartfelt sorrow for the mourners at the tomb, v. 35) as well as the divinity of our Lord (He commands the decayed dead and they obey, vv. 43–44). Point out the cause of death (sin; see Ezekiel 18:20; Romans 6:23) and its universal reign over all people (see Romans 5:12–19). Having moved the reader from Cana's wedding to Lazarus' resurrection near Bethany, John is now ready to move the reader into Passion Week. This second half of John's Gospel reveals God's solution to our problem: the cross. The epilogue (John 21) records Peter's return to his position of leadership among the apostles and the continued ministry of John after the other apostles had died,[8] both helpful pieces of information for the Early Church.

Example 3: Mark (Gospel)

Sometimes literary structures are harder to spot. John organized his Gospel in a way that most readers would see it. Mark, on the other hand, can be a little more difficult. Like seeing the wooden frame underneath the upholstery of a couch or a recliner, a reader sometimes has to come back to a text multiple times before its structure becomes apparent. Mark offers us a good example of a literary structure that lies unseen just below the surface of the story. **Keep comparing the different parts of the book to discover its deep structure and argument.**

Mark's first chapter shows how the Gospel of Jesus Christ, the Son of God, got off to a great start. John the Baptist prepared the way, then Jesus entered the wilderness after His Baptism by John, defeated Satan, and began His itinerant ministry in Galilee—all in fifteen verses! He then called His first disciples, exorcised a demon by a word of command (Mark 1:25), healed many (including Peter's mother-in-law), preached the Gospel, and then healed more sick people. By the end of the first chapter, Jesus seems to be unstoppable, overcoming every obstacle and quickly traveling down a path of sweet success. The next five dramatic scenes (Mark 2:1–3:6) show us a different picture.[9]

Scene 1: Jesus heals a paralytic, forgiving his sins as only God can do (2:1–12).

Scene 2: Jesus calls Levi and eats dinner with him and his friends (2:13–17).

Scene 3: Jesus handles a question about fasting and feasting (2:18–22).

Scene 4: Jesus defends His disciples when they pluck grain on the Sabbath (2:23–28).

Scene 5: Jesus heals a man with a withered hand on the Sabbath (3:1–6).

At first glance, these five stories seem to be no more than a series of conflicts that result in opposing political parties (the Herodians and the Pharisees) overcoming their differences for the purpose of killing Jesus (3:6). However, a closer look reveals a pattern. Scenes 1 and 5 involve healing. Scenes 2, 3, and 4 involve eating. In addition, scenes 1 and 2 share a theme of forgiveness, and scenes 4 and 5 were Sabbath violations according to the interpretation of Mosaic Law held by religious leaders at that time. This double "bookend" effect (sometimes called a *chiasmus*) emphasizes for the reader the importance of the material between the "bookends." In Mark 2:20, the center of that material, Jesus says, "The days will come when the bridegroom is taken away from them, and then they will fast in that day." The phrase "is taken away" appears only here and in the parallel passages (Matthew 9:15 and Luke 5:35) in the New Testament. Given the context, it's hard not to think of the cross here. If so, this would be the first Passion prediction in the Gospel, revealing Jesus' goal for His ministry—to give His life as a ransom for people (see Mark 10:45).

Mark then moves the reader through Jesus' ministry to Holy Week, where five questions or challenges reveal the stubborn unbelief of those who oppose Jesus and seek to take His life (Mark 11:27–12:37).

1. Religious leaders challenge Jesus' authority (Mark 11:27–33).
2. Pharisees and Herodians challenge Jesus on taxes (Mark 12:13–17).
3. Sadducees challenge the bodily resurrection (Mark 12:18–27).
4. An expert in the Hebrew Scriptures asks a legal question (Mark 12:28–34).
5. Jesus challenges His audience's messianic expectations (Mark 12:35–37).

The final question, asked by Jesus Himself (like the question asked by the head of the household at the Passover Seder[10]) in 12:35–37, highlights one of the problems we encounter when working with a translated text rather than the original. Jesus challenges His audience to reconsider their messianic expectations by quoting Psalm 110:1. Religious leaders of the day believed that the passage referred to the coming Messiah but did not notice the problem inherent in the verse. The problem does not show up in translation. We might translate as follows to catch something of the issue. David writes: "YAHWEH[11] said to my Master, sit at My right hand until I put Your enemies under Your feet" (author's translation). In that culture, respect went "uphill" not "downhill." You called your ancestors "sir" or "master" but never your children or descendants. How then could the great King David (who lived a thousand years earlier), say of his distant descendant, "my Master"? People looked longingly for the Messiah to come, but they thought of Him only as a human being. The concept of God Incarnate was utterly alien to them. How else, though, could King David call his distant descendant "my Master" or "my Lord" unless that distant descendant was more than merely human? Jesus sums up the problem: "David himself calls Him Lord. So how is He his son?" (Mark 12:37).

These literary structures at the beginning and at the end of Jesus' public ministry highlight the motivations of those who oppose Him but also reveal His intent and goal (the cross, where Jesus—God Incarnate—goes to give His life for the world). Like John, Mark has prepared his readers for Holy Week by putting together his account of Jesus' public ministry into a well-organized, structured "engine" that moves us to the Passion of our Lord.

Example 4: 1 Corinthians (Epistles)

Epistles, like the Old Testament Prophets, challenge the Bible study leader to do a little more homework than some of the other books in the Bible. Many books can be read as a sort of stand-alone document; we still need to know something of the geography, history, and culture reflected in those works, but they contain their own story (for example, Genesis and Matthew). That is, they contain a narrative that a reader can follow from beginning to end.

Reading an epistle (or, to some extent, an Old Testament prophet) is like listening to one side of a telephone conversation. We don't know what went on before the conversation started, we don't know what the other party is saying, and we may not know much about the topic under discussion. **Study leaders need to provide class members with some of the background to the epistle (or prophet) so that they can become part of the conversation in the epistle.** The Book of Acts offers indispensable information for people who read the New Testament Epistles.

Let's take 1 Corinthians as an example of how seeing the connections between parts of an epistle and understanding how the parts fit together helps the interpreter. Located about fifty miles southwest of Athens, just across the isthmus that connects the Peloponnese peninsula with the rest of Greece, Corinth has a very long history. After its destruction in 146 BC by the Romans, Julius Caesar had it rebuilt as a Roman colony shortly before his assassination in 44 BC. Luke records Paul's visit to Corinth on his second missionary journey (Acts 18:1–17; for a discussion of the events in Corinth, see Andrew Steinmann, *From Abraham to Paul: A Biblical Chronology* [Concordia, 2011], pp. 331–33). Either research on the Internet or a good Bible encyclopedia will provide a picture of Corinth at the time of Paul. To say that it was a difficult place to plant a church would be understating the challenge. Yet Paul and others labored eighteen months there (AD 50–51) to do just that. A few years later, writing from Ephesus (see 1 Corinthians 16:8) toward the end of Paul's third missionary journey, the apostle writes a series of letters to correct a variety of ethical and doctrinal problems in the Church at Corinth.[12] Problems in Corinth sprouted like weeds in a garden and, as with a garden, the weeds needed to be removed for the health of the garden. Those problems covered a wide spectrum of issues, including divisions within the church (1:10–4:21), moral transgressions (chs. 5–6), misunderstandings about marriage and idols (7:1–11:1), worship problems (11:2–14:40), and the resurrection (ch. 15).[13] Chapter 16 deals with "housekeeping items," such as a collection for the Jerusalem poor and Paul's travel plans.

We can demonstrate the value of recognizing the structure of an epistle by looking at the apparent contradiction between 1 Corinthians 11:5, where Paul requires a woman to wear a head covering[14] when praying in church or bringing a prophecy to the congregation, and 1 Corinthians 14:34–35, where Paul requires women to be silent. How can Paul say both things?

We begin by seeing 1 Corinthians 11:2–14:40 as a single unit. Paul establishes his theological foundation in 1 Corinthians 11:3, drawn especially from Genesis 1 and 2, and then addresses a series of issues: head coverings (reflecting the structure of marriage, 11:4–16), the Lord's Supper (embracing both the unity of the Church as the Body of Christ and the doctrine of the real presence, 11:17–34), and spiritual gifts (ch. 12). The apostle then reminds his readers that the key to solving their problems is love (ch. 13).[15] In chapter 14, he turns to the specific spiritual gifts of prophecy and tongues. He establishes a series of guidelines for the use of these gifts in public worship services:

1. The use of these gifts in public worship has one purpose: to build up the worshipers (as noted in 14:4).
2. Everyone who speaks in tongues much have an interpreter (14:13, 19).
3. Everything "should be done decently and in order" (14:40). At most, two or three people may speak in tongues or bring prophecies. Then the others present must judge the value of what is said (see 14:29).
4. During this evaluation, the women are to be silent, reflecting the structure of the male-female relationship as embodied in marriage (14:34).

The context shows us that Paul's instruction forbidding women to speak applies only to evaluating the interpretations of tongues and prophecies. This authority belongs to the men (or the male leadership) of the congregation (see also 1 Timothy 2:12). Only by ignoring the structure of this unit (1 Corinthians 11:2–14:40) and the immediate context of 14:34 can someone think that Paul contradicts himself in this book. For Paul, the Church of Jesus is family, and like a family, it operates according to God's design in Genesis 2.

Summary

In this chapter, we learned to begin our study by calling on the Lord in prayer, to read the text around our passage to be sure we understand the context, to watch for the author's purpose or goal, to examine the book's structure, to compare the parts of the book with one another, and to draw on background information.

To help you through any passage, be sure to use "A Checklist for Bible Study Preparation" found in appendix one on pages 187–189. It will walk you through step by step.

Chapter 18 Notes

1. Day 1, John 1:19–28; day 2, John 1:29–34; day 3, John 1:35–42; day 4, John 1:43–51; day 7 ("On the third day . . . ."), John 2:1.
2. The Greek word for "wine," *oinos*, denotes a beverage fermented from grapes with an alcohol content. Fermentation is crucial to Jesus' example in Mark 2:22 because carbon dioxide will expand a brittle, older wineskin to the point that it bursts—

losing both wine and container. The alcohol content of wine is also obvious from Jesus' comments in Luke 7:33–34. John the Baptist, subject to a lifelong Nazirite vow, could eat no grapes or grape products, including wine (see Numbers 6:2–3 for the Nazirite vow regulations; Luke 1:15 records the Nazirite prohibition given by the angel to John the Baptist's father, Zechariah). In both Mark 2:22 and Luke 7:33, the word in the original text is *oinos*.

3. The verb *sin* appears in the present tense in the original here, with the force of "stop sinning." The verb tense highlights the fact that the man who was healed was committing sin even as he stood in the temple, no doubt fulfilling his religious duties.
4. Sabbath laws were very important to people under the Mosaic covenant. Numbers 15:32–36 records the story of a man who picked up sticks for a fire on the Sabbath, completely disregarding God's command to rest. His punishment? Death. Because it was a sin done with full knowledge of God's command (see Numbers 15:30–31; a "high hand" means rebellious disregard), God applied the maximum penalty for intentional sin.
5. In John 6:20, as He walks on the rough seas of the lake, Jesus says to His disciples: "I Am; stop fearing" (author's translation). The phrase "I Am" in the original exactly duplicates the Septuagint's translation of God's covenant name in Exodus 3:14. We have no need to fear anything, for Jesus, our Savior, is Lord of all.
6. Jewish and Muslim traditions both emphasize a washing of the body and burial (without embalming) as soon as possible after death. In the first century and in most of the world today, the immediate burial of the dead is a very practical matter. Decomposition begins quickly in warm climates like Palestine.
7. Formal mourning with family and friends lasted seven days in the Jewish culture of the day. Some observant Jews practice this today.
8. A note that helps date the Gospel of John.
9. As noted by William L. Lane, *The Gospel of Mark* (Grand Rapids: Eerdmans, 1974).

10. William Lane, *The Gospel of Mark*, page 421, discusses the suggestion that these five questions parallel questions asked at the Passover Seder, a natural connection given the fact that Passover was only a few days away and that Jesus highly valued it.
11. Transliterated from the Hebrew form of God's covenant name, Exodus 3:14.
12. As far as we know, at least two letters to the Corinthians did not survive. Paul refers to a previous letter in 1 Corinthians 5:9, and he refers in 2 Corinthians 2:3–4 to a lost letter written between 1 and 2 Corinthians. His letter to the Laodiceans, mentioned in Colossians 4:16, is also lost.
13. See *The Lutheran Study Bible* (Concordia, 2009), page 1946, for more details.
14. Not only was it the custom for an adult woman to wear a head covering of some sort in the culture of Paul's day, but Paul anchors his requirement in the creation account of Genesis 2 and the theological statement of 1 Corinthians 11:3, which serves as the basis for the entire section of chapters 11–14. Because of our identity as the image of God, as men and women who reflect the glory of God, a woman must wear a head covering if she leads a prayer or brings a prophecy to the worship services in the Corinthian Church.
15. By "love," he has in mind the other-centered, Christ-like devotion to fellow Christians that sets aside pride and self-concern in mutual service to the saints. As leader of the Bible study, you may want to spend some time on distinguishing our culture's definition of love (a fleeting emotion) and love defined by the cross (see Romans 5:6–8).

Chapter 19

Lifting the Veil: A Look at the End Times or Eschatology

SOMETIMES PEOPLE MISINTERPRET A TEACHING FROM THE Bible, but the idea seems so appealing that millions of Christians accept it. One of the hardest things a Bible reader needs to do is set aside as many preconceptions as possible before opening Scripture and reading a text. The three topics in this chapter illustrate that challenge. As you work through them, ask yourself which principles of interpretation will “sort the wheat from the chaff” that is, separate truth from falsehood.

The Temple

When the Lord established a covenant at Mount Sinai with the people He brought out of Egypt, He also gave instructions through Moses about the tabernacle, its priesthood, and its furnishings (Exodus 25–40). The tabernacle served as a portable “embassy” where the Lord and His people could come together through the agency of the Levitical priesthood. The tabernacle housed the “ambassador’s seat,” the ark of the covenant, in the Most Holy Place at the center of the tabernacle (Exodus 26:33–34). Solomon, the last king to rule over a united Israel, built the temple in Jerusalem to replace the tabernacle (1 Kings 6; 967–960 BC). Known as the “first temple,” Solomon’s temple stood until razed by the Babylonians in 587 BC.[1] Those who returned from exile in Babylon eventually rebuilt the Jerusalem temple around 516 BC (Ezra 6–7). This second temple never compared in beauty and majesty to the first temple.[2] In fact, when it was finished, those who remembered the first temple wept (Ezra 3:12–13).

Herod the Great began to rebuild the temple in 20 BC. He wanted to make it a magnificent edifice, something by which later generations would remember him. Although work continued for another eighty years or so, it was largely finished within a year and a half. It must have been truly impressive, for even the disciples of Jesus (who had often visited the temple) remarked on its beauty (see Matthew 24:1; Luke 21:5). When Jerusalem fell to the Romans in AD 70, the invaders destroyed the temple, and it was never rebuilt. When Islam swept into the city in the seventh century AD, a mosque was constructed on the Temple Mount.

Some Christians believe the temple will be rebuilt, a Levitical priesthood will be reestablished, and sacrifices will once again commence in this rebuilt temple. Often connected to a belief that Jesus will reign for one thousand years in Jerusalem before the final judgment (see ch. 11, "Apocalyptic Writings"), we need to ask if there's a genuine biblical basis for another temple in Jerusalem. Those who look for a new temple also look for a red heifer from whose ashes the water for purification can be made (see Numbers 19). These purifying waters will be used to cleanse or sanctify the new temple, the priests, and the garments and furniture used in the temple. It sounds pretty exciting, but is it real? Does the Bible predict another temple in Jerusalem?

It is true that the New Testament contains a reference to Numbers 19 and the red heifer. The author of Hebrews contrasts the purification water made with the ashes of the red heifer with the blood of Christ (Hebrews 9:13–14). The argument in the verses moves from the lesser (the water of purification) to the greater (the blood of Jesus). The lesser (the temple and its sacrifices) has passed away; the greater, Jesus Christ, has come and accomplished what the temple and the Law could not—the forgiveness of sins. Jesus' sacrifice, offered once for all, ended the need for any other sacrifice (Hebrews 10:8–10). According to the author of Hebrews, reinstituting the Mosaic system of sacrifices (including the purifying waters made from the red heifer) would deny the cross of Christ and nullify His "once for all" effective sacrifice.

The author of Hebrews also helps us understand the significance and role of the temple (and the tabernacle that preceded it). In Hebrews 9:24–25, he refers to the tabernacle and the temple as "copies" of a heavenly original. The two words used in the original text of these verses refer to a pattern or model that corresponds to the original. This picture of the temple allows us to think of it as an embassy. Here on earth, when we enter the embassy of a foreign government we are then on the soil of that foreign country. The embassy may be located in our country and, to some extent, under our jurisdiction, but it is also an extension of that foreign county. It is a copy or a model corresponding to the original.

If the tabernacle and its replacement serve as merely a model of the heavenly reality, what does Scripture say of that reality? Our first clue appears in Matthew 12:5–6. In a disagreement with Jewish leaders over what is and what is not permitted on the Sabbath, Jesus states, "Or have you not read in the Law how on the Sabbath the priests in the temple profane the Sabbath and are guiltless? I tell you, something greater than the temple is here." Does Jesus regard Himself as greater than the Jerusalem temple? It would appear that He does, particularly in light of His statement in Matthew 12:8: "For the Son of Man" (meaning Himself) "is lord of the Sabbath." In this statement, Jesus claims the authority to judge what is "in bounds" and "out of bounds" on the Sabbath, a divine authority (see Daniel 7:13–14 as His source for "Son of Man").

We have a second clue regarding the relationship between Jesus and the Jerusalem temple. When challenged by the Jewish leadership to provide authorization for cleansing the temple in John 2, Jesus replied, "Destroy this temple, and in three days I will raise it up" (v. 19). His resurrection will provide the proof that He has the authority to cleanse the temple (similar to the "sign of Jonah" in Matthew 16:4). The fact that Jesus rose from the dead publicly vindicates His claim to be the Messiah—the incarnate Son of God and Savior of the world. It helps us in our present investigation of the temple because Jesus here refers to *Himself* as the temple. This claim made a real impact on those who heard it. Not only do His accusers bring it up at His trial before the high priest (Matthew 26:61; Mark 14:58) but His enemies use it to mock Him when He is on the cross (Matthew 27:40). If the temple serves only as a promise of things to come, Jesus fulfills that promise. He is the heavenly reality that renders the temple obsolete, demonstrated by the tearing of the curtain in the temple when Jesus died on the cross (Matthew 27:51; Mark 15:38; Luke 23:45). Jesus destroys the barrier between God and mankind by paying the ultimate sacrifice for the sins of the world.

Stephen, the first martyr, understood this. As he preached the Gospel of Jesus Christ, he pointed out the impact of Christ's sacrifice and resurrection on our relationship to the Mosaic Law as well as its significance for the Jerusalem temple. His accusers said, "This man never ceases to speak words against this holy place and the law, for we have heard him say that this Jesus of Nazareth will destroy this place and will change the customs that Moses delivered to us" (Acts 6:13–14). At his trial, Stephen points out the fact that the God of Israel has never been confined to any building built by human hands (Acts 7:48) and that God's people have never kept the Law (Acts 7:52–53). For his honesty, they stoned him to death.

Yet, he was right. Baptized into Christ, we died to the Law and are free to live for Him (Romans 6:1–4; 7:4). To require obedience to the Law (even circumcision) nullifies the Gospel (Paul's argument in Galatians). This leads the reader of Scripture to the following conclusion: Rebuilding the temple would be an act of idolatry, denying Jesus as the one greater than the temple. Reinstituting the Mosaic system of sacrifices (including the purifying waters made with the ashes of the red heifer) would deny the cross as the one sacrifice that takes away the sins of the whole world.

Some of those who defend the theory of a new temple point to four passages to support their position.

1. Daniel 9:27 is part of a challenging text (Daniel 9:24–27) where the imagery of the temple is used to describe the violent persecutions of God's people in the short time just prior to the final judgment. (See the chart on p. 1417 of *The Lutheran Study Bible* [Concordia, 2009].)
2. Matthew 24:15 refers to Daniel's figure of the "abomination of desolation" (the offensive thing that drives people out) in Daniel 11:31 and 12:11. This prediction was initially fulfilled when Antiochus Epiphanes built an altar to Zeus in the Jerusalem temple and offered a pig as a sacrifice around 168 BC. Jesus warns His followers in Matthew 24:15–16 (see also Mark 13:14) to flee the city when they see a similar sacrilege in the temple. During the Roman siege of Jerusalem (AD 66–70), zealots committed a number of atrocities within the temple precincts. The Roman siege briefly lifted at one point because Vespasian left for Rome. (He became emperor in AD 69.) His son, Titus, reinstituted the siege shortly thereafter, but a large number of Christians in the city, responding to Jesus' warnings,

left and hid in the hills (according to Eusebius, a fourth-century Church historian).

3. 2 Thessalonians 2:3–4 has Paul picturing the "man of lawlessness" (see the next section in this chapter) as sitting in the temple of God. We might note that no one "sat" in the Jerusalem temple. This suggests Paul is using "temple" as a symbol, an observation confirmed by the use of the Greek word *naos* ("sanctuary, inner part of the temple") rather than *hieros* (the temple as a whole) in this verse. The second half of 2 Thessalonians 2:4 (sitting in the sanctuary) simply repeats in a visual way the point of the first half of the verse, that the "man of lawlessness" will exalt himself above every god or object of worship.
4. Revelation 11:1 says John is told to measure the "temple of God" (again, *naos* rather than *hieros*) with a measuring rod like a staff. It is clear from the contents of Revelation 11 that God's concern is for His people, not the building (which was destroyed by the Romans in AD 70). No one can harm His people (the purpose of measuring them) during the time of Gentile outreach (the New Testament age, Matthew 28:16–20). God does not promise that His people will not suffer and die for the faith. Rather, He promises that no one and nothing can snatch them out of His hand (John 10:27–29; Romans 8:28–39). We might also remember that the real temple of God is Jesus Christ and that we, baptized into Him, are living stones built into a spiritual house (1 Peter 2:4–5).

Christians, therefore, should not look for a new temple in Jerusalem. Such an expectation rests on a misunderstanding of Jesus and a confusion of Law and Gospel. It ignores the testimony of clear Scripture.

What steps did we take to arrive at our conclusion regarding the rebuilding of the temple?

1. We did a word search (using a concordance or computer software) on *heifer* and *tabernacle/temple*, looking at the passages to determine the following:
    a. What was its purpose or function under Mosaic Law?
    b. What use does the New Testament make of it?

2. We looked at a variety of websites supported by proponents of the new temple theory, trying to determine how it fit into their picture of the end times and identifying passages used to support their position.
3. We considered the points raised by Stephen (Acts 7) and the contrast between the old and new covenants developed by the author of Hebrews. These clear Scripture passages provided a framework for evaluating the new temple theory.
4. We examined the texts used to support the new temple in the original contexts of each text and found they did not support the rebuilding of the temple.
5. In the light of the analogy of faith, the testimony of clear passages in Scripture, and the distinction between Law and Gospel, we concluded that the rebuilt temple theory is contrary to Scripture as well as the person and work of Jesus Christ.

The Antichrist

Who or what is the "Antichrist"? A quick search in a good Bible dictionary, encyclopedia, or an online resource (such as www.theopedia.com) will likely provide a broad spectrum of answers. These resources can also provide the student of Scripture with a number of passages that relate to the question but don't actually use the term *antichrist*. As noted earlier, word searches in translations can be problematic—a receptor language may use a variety of terms to translate a single word in the original. The receptor language may also use a single word to translate several different terms in the original. However, a basic word search is a great place to start. The second step we take, checking a dictionary, encyclopedia, or looking online, allows us to look at other places in Scripture where the same subject appears but without the particular word we searched.

Our word search on *antichrist* shows that it appears four times in the Bible:

1 John 2:18, "Children, it is the last hour, and as you have heard that antichrist is coming, so now many antichrists have come."

1 John 2:22, "Who is the liar but he who denies that Jesus is the Christ? This is the antichrist, he who denies the Father and the Son."

> 1 John 4:2–3, "By this you know the Spirit of God: every spirit that confesses that Jesus Christ has come in the flesh is from God, and every spirit that does not confess Jesus is not from God. This is the spirit of the antichrist, which you heard was coming and now is in the world already."
>
> 2 John 1:7, "For many deceivers have gone out into the world, those who do not confess the coming of Jesus Christ in the flesh. Such a one is the deceiver and the antichrist."

Several points become clear as a result of the word search. First, *antichrist* refers to more than one person. Second, antichrists seek to deceive believers, denying the real Jesus (truly God and truly man) and replacing Him with a phony substitute. (Closely connected to this denial of Christ as God Incarnate is the rejection of the Trinity.) Third, the spirit of antichrists opposes the Spirit of Christ. This identifies the power behind antichrists as the devil, whose first attack on God's children was through deception (Genesis 3:1–6). Throughout the New Testament era, believers need to be on guard against those who teach a different Jesus than Scripture reveals, for those false teachers will be a constant threat to the salvation of Christ's people. Jesus warns us about these false teachers and the dangers they present in Matthew 24 (as noted above in ch. 11 under "Guidelines for Understanding Apocalyptic Writing").

In Matthew 24, Jesus provides His disciples a snapshot of the temple's destruction (which took place a little less than forty years later) and uses this as a lens to show us something of the New Testament age and its culmination shortly before the final judgment. Jesus uses Daniel's figure of "the abomination that makes desolate" (Daniel 11:31; 12:11) to warn His followers to flee Jerusalem (Matthew 24:15–16). Daniel's prophecy found fulfillment in 167 BC when Antiochus IV Epiphanes sacrificed pigs to the god Zeus in the Jerusalem temple compound. When similar sacrileges occur in the temple compound (which they did during the siege of Jerusalem, AD 66–70), Jesus warns, "Head for the hills!" Will a similar abomination appear at the end of the New Testament age?

Christians will face both persecution (see Matthew 24:9–12) as well as deception (as in Matthew 24:23–28) throughout the New Testament era. John's vision of the opposition faced by believers in Revelation 13 depicts these two forces as two beasts, both of which work throughout the time between Jesus' first and second comings. The first beast, the beast from the sea, represents political oppression and physical persecution (Revelation 13:1–10). Facing this sort of trial, John challenges Christians to accept captivity and execution if that is necessary. "Here is a call for the endurance and faith of the saints" (Revelation 13:10). The second beast, the beast from the land (fulfilling the pattern of antichrist), seeks to deceive people on earth. Surviving this beast requires wisdom, perceiving the sinful desire to be like God (Genesis 3:5, symbolized by *666* in Revelation 13:18) that lies at the heart of its deception.[3] The two beasts are closely connected to each other—oppressive governments often claim religious power over their subjects and deceptive religions frequently manipulate the government for their own purposes. Satan directs both beasts with the goal of destroying God's people (Revelation 12:17).

So far, our investigation of *antichrist* has revealed that the word does not refer to only a specific person but to a whole pattern of opposition to Jesus Christ and His Church. Anyone who denies the Trinity (Father, Son, Holy Spirit—one God) or the person and work of Jesus Christ (particularly the incarnation) is "antichrist." This pattern of hostility and deception has been present since the earliest days of the Church and will continue throughout the New Testament age. Christians of every generation need to be on guard against false teachers who would substitute a "fake" Jesus for the real one. Before we leave the subject of *antichrist*, however, we may want to ask whether Scripture says anything about a single figure that appears at the end of this age to do the work of Satan.

We find just such a figure in 2 Thessalonians 2:1–12. Like the believers at Corinth (evidenced in 1 Corinthians 7 and 15), Christians at Thessalonica are confused about the nature of the New Testament age. They realize that the end times have begun in the person and work of Jesus Christ and the outpouring of the Holy Spirit on Pentecost, but they don't realize that the actual end of the age and the final judgment lie in the future.[4] The Day of the Lord (that is, the ultimate victory of Christ over all the forces that oppose Him) is still a future event (see 1 Corinthians 15:25; compare 2 Thessalonians 2:2–3).

At the end of the New Testament era, not long before the final judgment of the world by Jesus Christ, there will be a great "apostasy" or "rebellion" on earth (2 Thessalonians 2:3–4). At that time, the "man of lawlessness"[5] will be revealed, a figure doomed to destruction. (*Son of destruction* means "one who embodies the characteristic of destruction.") He stands as the ultimate "Antichrist," claiming both divine and secular authority.

Lawlessness serves as something of a technical term for rebellion against God and His design for creation (see Matthew 24:12). This rebellion continues throughout the New Testament age but remains subdued while the Holy Spirit works to bring people to faith in Christ through the spread of the Gospel. At the end, the "man of lawlessness" will be revealed, and persecution of Christians will increase dramatically (Matthew 24:21–24).

It is important to note that people will not be able to figure out the identity of this individual until the right moment. He will be revealed by God for what he is, an agent of Satan who tries to destroy the Church but, in the end, is himself destroyed (2 Thessalonians 2:7–10). Satan works through him (he is "energized" by Satan, v. 9) to attack the children of God. The solution for the Church? "So then, brothers, stand firm and hold to the traditions that you were taught by us, either by our spoken word or by our letter" (2 Thessalonians 2:15). These traditions[6] are the doctrines handed down to them from Paul and the other apostles (just like in 1 Corinthians 15:1–11).

What tools and what principles have we used in our investigation of *antichrist*?

1. We began with a word search (using a concordance or appropriate software).
2. We looked at the topic in other resources (Bible dictionary, Bible encyclopedia, Internet search engine).
3. We read the relevant passages, paying close attention to context.
4. When reading passages from apocalyptic literature (such as Revelation), we remember the code: symbolic use of numbers, vivid imagery, frequent use of Old Testament background.
5. We looked at related passages that spoke to the topic (such as 2 Thessalonians 2). We discovered these passages from previous Bible reading sessions and from encyclopedias and Internet websites.
6. We drew our conclusions, accounting for all the evidence and using Matthew 24 as "control" material (the clear passages help us interpret the unclear ones).

The So-Called "Rapture"

Will Christians have to endure terrible persecutions at the end or will they be evacuated before it gets really ugly?

A quick check of a Bible encyclopedia or an Internet search reveals that, for some Christians, one primary text used in researching this question is 1 Thessalonians 4:13–18. Other passages, such as Matthew 24:36–44, sometimes appear in discussions of this topic as well. We discover two schools of thought regarding these passages: They are either thought to be part of the general resurrection at the end of time, or they are seen as the evacuation of Christians prior to (or sometimes in the middle of) the last, terrible period of persecution (sometimes called "the great tribulation").

We begin by reading 1 Thessalonians 4:13–18. Having written the letter very early (AD 50 or 51), Paul writes to correct a number of misunderstandings among the believers in Thessalonica. The question he addresses in these verses is fairly straightforward: will those who die[7] before the Lord's return suffer any disadvantage compared to those who are still alive when He returns (1 Thessalonians 4:15)? Paul assures his readers that living believers will not enjoy any advantage over those who have died because both those who are alive and those who are dead will be "caught up" ("raptured") together "to meet the Lord in the air" (1 Thessalonians 4:17).

Clearly, Paul has in mind the events of Judgment Day. He writes to people who expected the imminent return of Christ Jesus and wants them to understand that those believers who die before His return will not miss out on anything. We see once more the importance of context in reading Scripture. Paul does not write about a great tribulation here, nor does he offer believers any false hope of escaping persecution at the end. He simply points out to Christians that we need not worry about fellow believers who die before the Lord's return in glory to judge the living and the dead. This leads us to conclude that those who look for an evacuation prior to the great tribulation (or in the middle of it) have misunderstood Scripture. Those who believe they will be raptured away before the persecution begins (or before it gets really bad) may find their faith tested when that doesn't happen.

Can we confirm our understanding of the rapture by looking at other places in Scripture that speak to questions of suffering and resurrection? We might remember the High Priestly Prayer of Jesus in John 17. As our Lord finishes His ministry here on earth, He prays for His followers then and now. He prays, "I do not ask that You take them out of the world, but that You keep them from the evil one" (John 17:15). Our Lord calls His disciples to follow Him, even if it means rejection, suffering, and death (Luke 9:23; 14:27).

Another helpful section of Scripture is the "great resurrection chapter," 1 Corinthians 15. In 1 Corinthians 15:23–24, Paul pictures three distinct phases of the resurrection: (1) the resurrection of Jesus Christ, the "firstfruits"; (2) the resurrection of believers, both those alive and those who have fallen asleep; (3) the general resurrection of the unbelievers, followed by the final judgment. Our conclusions regarding the rapture in 1 Thessalonians 4 fit this framework very well. The second phase of the resurrection would then be what Paul has in mind when he writes about the general resurrection.

We might even call to mind the triumphal entry of our Savior when He entered Jerusalem in humility (Matthew 21:1–11), headed to the cross to lay down His life for the sins of the world. Not only did His disciples follow Him, but a large crowd came out of Jerusalem with palm branches and shouts of praise to celebrate His arrival (John 12:12–13). The Last Day may well be similar, a scene of great joy as Jesus returns in glory to judge all humanity, greeted in the air by believers, followed by the final judgment (see Revelation 19:11–21 for a very vivid picture of this).

When we consider passages used to support other views of a rapture (e.g., a pre- or mid-tribulation rapture), such as Matthew 24:36–44, we find that these passages do not speak to the question of the rapture at all. In Matthew, Jesus tells His followers to be ready at all times for the end. He uses the story of Noah and the ark to illustrate the need for watchfulness and faithful living. The end will come suddenly, so that some will be taken and some will be left. Ordinarily, those who are taken by an invading force suffer a bitter fate: slavery, exile, and death in a foreign land. If that is the background for Jesus' comments in Matthew 24:40–41, then the ones left behind are the fortunate ones; but that is not the case! In summary, our Savior's instructions in these verses don't speak directly to a rapture and should not be pressed to mean something He does not say.

What principles have we used in this investigation?

1. Remembered to stick with the plain and simple meaning of the text.
2. Looked closely at the immediate context and let that inform our reading of the passage.
3. Compared our interpretation with other parts of Scripture.

Chapter 19 Notes

1. Search the Internet or a good study Bible to find an illustration of Solomon's temple (for example, p. 541 of *The Lutheran Study Bible* [Concordia, 2009]); then spend a few minutes considering what the temple would have looked like and what impact it would have made on those who entered it.
2. Compare the drawing on page 730 of the second temple (Zerubbabel's temple) in *The Lutheran Study Bible* with the drawing of the first temple on page 541.
3. Remember that Roman emperors of this period, like eastern monarchs, claimed to be divine and required worship by their subjects. See also the discussion of Revelation 13:18 in chapter 15 under "The Living Bible" in the section on paraphrases.
4. Sometimes called "over-realized eschatology," a focus on the spiritual reign of God now to the exclusion of the physical end of the world and the judgment that follows.
5. The King James Version has "man of sin," reflecting a somewhat later manuscript tradition. There is no substantive difference, since "lawlessness" is a variety of sin (see 1 John 3:4).
6. A "tradition" as used in 2 Thessalonians 2 and 1 Corinthians 15 refers to that body of teaching that is handed down from teacher to student or from one generation to another.
7. Paul uses the phrase "fallen asleep" when he refers to the death of believers (1 Corinthians 15:6, 18, 20; 1 Thessalonians 4:15 [our passage]; 5:10). He does not imply a "soul sleep" but uses "fallen asleep" as an appropriate analogy. Just as we lay down to sleep and wake up again, so believers will lie down in their graves but arise when Jesus returns to judge the living and the dead. Paul does not use "fallen asleep" of nonbelievers because they will rise to judgment rather than life with the Lord. Scripture clearly teaches that believers enter God's presence at the moment of death (Luke 23:43) and may be conscious of their location and of time passing on earth (Revelation 6:9–11).

Chapter 20

Following Your Nose

HAVE YOU EVER WALKED INTO A PLACE AND SMELLED SOMEthing good? Baking bread, for example, sends out its wonderful aroma so that even those passing by in the street notice it and enjoy the moment. Reading the Bible can be like that. We might be looking at one passage and come across something that, like baking bread, catches our attention and curiosity. If it's possible, take the time to "follow your nose" and see where it leads. Sometimes those chance discoveries shed a new light on a familiar passage or take us to a passage we haven't really read before. In this chapter, we will review three fragrant passages that invite us to a feast of biblical blessings.

Seventy Seventies

Let us suppose that we are researching the Bible's teaching on the subject of forgiveness. Sooner or later, we will run across Matthew 18:21–22, "Then Peter came up and said to Him, 'Lord, how often will my brother sin against me, and I forgive him? As many as seven times?' Jesus said to him, 'I do not say to you seven times, but seventy-seven times'" (some English translations have "seventy times seven"). This seems like a lot of forgiveness to offer, particularly because human beings aren't all that forgiving to start with. As the eighteenth-century poet, Alexander Pope, wrote, "To err is human; to forgive, divine."

You may take a moment to ask if there's anything else quite like this in Scripture. A quick word search seems in order. However, since different English translations offer a variety of numbers, it's a good idea to check several concordances or use a selection of terms in your Bible software: "seventy-seven times" generates the parallel of Genesis 4:24 in the NIV. That may not show up in a word search of other versions. For example, if you searched the NKJV's Matthew 18:22 rendering of "seventy times seven," you would not find Genesis 4:24 as a parallel passage since the NKJV uses "seventy-sevenfold" in that passage. If your software or skills permit, checking the original Greek of Matthew 18:22 and the Septuagint of Genesis 4:24 reveals the two phrases are identical—the only two places in the entire Greek Bible where that phrase appears.

Is this merely a coincidence, or is there a real connection?

As always, we look to the context to help provide the answer. Genesis 4 contains the story of Adam and Eve's family, beginning with Cain and Abel. When God confronts Cain after he murders Abel, Cain recoils at the punishment and expresses a concern that someone will kill him (as he killed Abel). God reassures Cain that this will not happen: "Not so! If anyone kills Cain, vengeance shall be taken on him sevenfold" (Genesis 4:15a). In other words, God demonstrates His power and authority over Cain's fate by promising a sevenfold payback for any attack on Cain.

Genesis tracks the family of Adam and Eve through Cain's side first (Seth's side appears in Genesis 4:25 and following). The seventh generation of mankind on Cain's side is Lamech, the first man to have two wives, Adah and Zillah (Genesis 4:19). If Adam and Eve were ashamed of their sin (Genesis 3:8) and Cain was surly and disrespectful when God confronted him about his sin (Genesis 4:9), Lamech shows us what sin looks like when it is fully mature—arrogant and prideful, claiming greater authority and power than God Himself. "Adah and Zillah, hear my voice; you wives of Lamech, listen to what I say: I have killed a man for wounding me, a young man for striking me. If Cain's revenge is sevenfold, then Lamech's is seventy-sevenfold" (Genesis 4:23–24).[1]

Both "seven" and "seventy-seven" appear in Genesis 4:24 and Matthew 18:22. In Genesis 4:24, we see the fulfillment of a progression begun in Genesis 3:1–6: sin grows up. The seventh generation of mankind on Cain's side shows the fullness (thus "seven," a number often connected to the full measure of something) of inherited sin.[2] Because of our sin, we imagine ourselves above God. Contrast Genesis 4:24 with Matthew 18:22. Peter's "seven times" falls far short of the divine standard. God wants His children to forgive others as He forgives them, without limit (compare the fifth petition of the Lord's Prayer, Matthew 6:12, 14–15). Jesus challenges Peter (and all His disciples) to forgive others as a normal practice without restriction, just as God forgives us for Jesus' sake (see Matthew 18:21–22). He then tells the story of the unforgiving servant (Matthew 18:23–35) to impress upon His followers that refusing to forgive others will cost us our own forgiveness. The only way to keep forgiveness, it seems, is to give it away.

Son of Jonah

Another example of "follow your nose" as a tool for Bible study can be given in Matthew 16:17. Peter confesses Jesus to be the Christ, the Son of the living God, and Jesus responds: "Blessed are you, Simon Bar-Jonah![3] For flesh and blood has not revealed this to you, but my Father who is in heaven." However, a quick search of *Simon Peter* in a dictionary, encyclopedia, or online will reveal that Simon Peter's father's name is John, not Jonah. What is more, we know that Jesus knows that because He addresses Peter as "son of John" when He calls Peter to follow Him (see John 1:42; 21:15–17).

Once again, a basic word search offers a great place to begin. We find a reference to the Old Testament prophet Jonah in 2 Kings 14:25, helping us to date the prophet to the reign of Jeroboam II in the eighth century BC. The rest of the references to Jonah in the Hebrew Scriptures appear in the short book that bears his name. His story is a simple one. God told him to go east, so he went west. Along the way, he found out you can't run away from God because God is everywhere. After being thrown overboard, a large sea creature swallowed Jonah and then returned him to dry land. He did travel east but was deeply angry with God because God had mercy on a terrible enemy of Israel, the Assyrians.

The part of the story that stands out for modern readers is that Jonah spent three days inside a large sea creature and lived to tell the tale. Fact or fiction? Nothing in the story of Jonah suggests it is anything other than factual.

The next time we encounter the story of Jonah is in Matthew 12:38–42. Faced with pressure to produce a sign for His adversaries, Jesus states: "An evil and adulterous generation seeks for a sign, but no sign will be given to it except the sign of the prophet Jonah. For just as Jonah was three days and three nights in the belly of the great fish, so will the Son of

Man be three days and three nights in the heart of the earth" (Matthew 12:39–40). Jesus certainly appears to take the story of Jonah at face value and goes so far as to use it as a template for His own upcoming burial and resurrection. Factual, indeed!

The next place our word search on Jonah takes us is Matthew 16:4, where Jesus once more makes the point that the only sign His adversaries will receive to authenticate His claim to be the Messiah will be His own resurrection, the "sign of Jonah" who reappeared after three days in the great sea creature. Given the close proximity of Matthew 16:4 to Matthew 16:17, and given the fact that Jesus knows full well the name of Simon's father (John), can we doubt that "son of[4] Jonah" is a reference to the faith of Peter in Jesus as the Christ, the Son of the living God? In his role as confessor, Peter takes on the resurrection character—eternal life revealed in Christ Jesus as a gift from our heavenly Father. Jesus builds His Church on this revelation, a Church that even death cannot destroy.

Matthew's Genealogy

Most people find a genealogy fascinating—if it is of their own family. Genealogies of other families may not hold much interest to most readers. It is possible, therefore, that many who begin to read Matthew skip the genealogy (1:1–17) and start with the birth of Jesus (1:18–25). It might seem like a good idea to skip all the names, especially since Matthew summarizes the genealogy in 1:17 (fourteen generations between each of the main figures: Abraham, David, Babylonian exile, and the birth of Jesus). Dividing the generations into units of seven, Jesus begins the seventh seven-generation unit (seven indicates fullness). The point: Jesus fulfills the messianic promise made to Abraham, ratified with David, kept intact through the exile, and implemented at Bethlehem.

However, there are four unusual names that should alert the reader to something else. If we "follow our nose," we'll find that each one of them presents a wonderful picture of God's grace at work as He moves the promise from one generation to another. All four are women, but none of them are what a person might expect in the family tree of God's Holy Son.

Tamar, Matthew 1:3

Genesis 38 records the story of Tamar. Probably a Canaanite rather than a Hebrew, she married Judah's oldest son, Er. When he died at the hand of God, she married Judah's second son, Onan. He also died under the justice of God. Judah promised she could marry his third and last son, Shelah, but it became obvious that Judah had no intention of risking his last child with this "black widow." Tamar took matters into her own hands, dressing up like a prostitute and waiting on the road where she knew her father-in-law, Judah, would pass. He had sex with her and made a deal with her for payment, but when payment arrived, she had disappeared. Tamar later turned up pregnant, a death-penalty mistake on her part—except that the father of her child was her father-in-law. (The Bible is typically regarded as a collection of stories for nice church-going folks, but bear in mind that more than a few Old Testament stories are shocking.) One of the twins she bore became ancestor to the Messiah. Question: Why would Matthew include such an ancestor as Tamar in this genealogy?

Rahab, Matthew 1:5

Rahab's story comes from the early conquest of Canaan by Joshua in Joshua 2. She lived in Jericho, a strategically important city on the Jordan River north of Jerusalem. She operated an inn, so it was a good place for the Hebrew spies to visit on their intelligence-gathering mission prior to the invasion. Apparently, Rahab provided other services as well, clearly identified as a prostitute by the author of Hebrews (11:31; public inns often had poor reputations in the ancient world). As a Canaanite, she would have been killed along with her family and the others in Jericho except that the Lord and Joshua spared her, due to her faith. She believed the God of the Hebrews would give them victory over her city, hid the spies, and saved herself and her family (see Joshua 2:15–21; James 2:25). More than that, she married a Hebrew and gave birth to a boy, Boaz, becoming an ancestor of the Messiah. Question: Why would Matthew include her in this genealogy?

Ruth, Matthew 1:5

We read about Ruth in the short book that bears her name. Outside of that book and this reference in Matthew 1:5, she does not appear in Scripture. Like Tamar and Rahab, she comes from a people group other than the Hebrews. As a Moabite, she could trace her ancestry back to Lot, Abraham's nephew. Genesis 19:31–36 records the shameful story of Ruth's family tree. Add to that embarrassment the fact that she was previously married before her union with Boaz, and we might think she would be intentionally omitted in any family history. Yet she married Boaz, an older man, and gave birth to Obed, becoming an ancestor of the Messiah. Question: Why would Matthew include her in this genealogy?

The Wife of Uriah, Matthew 1:6

Matthew does not even mention Bathsheba by name, but underscores the terrible events of 2 Samuel 11 by referring to her as simply "the wife of Uriah." A Hittite by birth, Uriah had come to believe in the one true God and stood side by side with his king, David, in many battles. Part of a true "band of brothers," he had laid his life on the line for many years in service to his king. David repays this tremendous loyalty and strong bond by engaging in an affair with Uriah's wife, Bathsheba (a death penalty crime for both of them). She became pregnant by David, and when David's efforts to cover it up by shifting responsibility to Uriah failed, David had Uriah and several of his other loyal bodyguards killed. Although that child died shortly after birth, their second child, Solomon, became king over Israel. Question: Why would Matthew include Bathsheba in this genealogy?

In his Gospel, Matthew wants to present Jesus as the Christ—the fulfillment of the messianic promises that stretch back to Abraham. He needs to document the genealogy of Jesus to authenticate His messianic kingship, fulfilling the line of promise as it moved from one generation to another (Abraham, Isaac, Jacob, Judah, and so forth). Why did he pick these four women to include in this genealogy?

We find the answer highlighted in Matthew 12:15–21 (citing Isaiah 42:1–3), where Gentiles are specifically included in the mission of the Messiah. When Jesus died, He died for all. He died for Jews as well as Gentiles, for "righteous" as well as "sinners." Even in Matthew's genealogy, we get a hint of the broad scope of God's love in Christ Jesus. The God of the Jews sent His Son, born of a Jewish woman, in the homeland of the Jewish people, to die for the sins of *all* people.

Researching these four women could be done with a simple word search by name, by checking a dictionary or Bible encyclopedia, or by looking online. The purpose of this chapter is to encourage your curiosity and invite you to take the time to "follow your nose" if you run into something that sticks out or seems a little different. Check your results with the context of the passage, the context of Scripture, and the analogy of faith to make sure you haven't come to the wrong conclusion. Remember, however, reading the Scripture is an adventure—filled with unexpected twists and turns, surprising humor, tremendous pathos, and real-life people and situations.

Chapter 20 Notes

1. Lamech boasts of more than "getting even." He will not be satisfied with "an eye for an eye" or a "tooth for a tooth" (the limit of retribution, Exodus 21:23–25). Commentators on Genesis, such as Gordon J. Wenham (*Word Biblical Commentary: Genesis 1–15* [Waco: Word Books, 1987], p. 114), have pointed out the contrast between God's justice in Exodus 21 and sinful man's vengeance in Genesis 4. Like an early incidence of road rage, Lamech threatens to kill a person for the equivalent of cutting him off in traffic.
2. The seventh generation of mankind on Seth's side (the godly side) is Enoch, who shows us the fullness of faith and faithfulness—"Thus all the days of Enoch were 365 years. Enoch walked with God, and he was not, for God took him" (Genesis 5:23–24).
3. "Bar" is Aramaic for "son." Jesus here addresses Peter as "Simon son of Jonah." Some translations (e.g., NIV, NRSV) render it that way.
4. Remember that "son of" means "has the character of, resembles."

Chapter 21

Learning from the History of Interpretation

HAVING LEARNED THE SEVEN PRINCIPLES OF INTERPRETATION and put them into practice, we may also gain great understanding from learning how previous generations of Christians have turned to the Bible for help in their lives. In history, we find examples to follow and examples that warn us not to repeat other people's mistakes. This chapter begins with the writers of the New Testament and the way they and their contemporaries read the Old Testament.

The New Testament

The earliest Christians to read Scripture and interpret it were the inspired authors of the New Testament. They read the Hebrew Scriptures and used a variety of rules (hermeneutics) to understand and apply the Word of God to Jesus, His mission and ministry, and to the life of His people.

Some New Testament writers had no training in the rabbinic schools (such as Peter and John, Acts 4:13). Others showed familiarity with the rules used by rabbis to read and understand the Hebrew Scriptures (such as Paul, Acts 22:3; see Acts 5:34). The famous Rabbi Hillel (first century BC) identified seven principles for reading Holy Scripture. His first rule (*kal va-chomer*) might be best understood as an argument from the lesser to the greater or vice versa. If something is true, then its greater (or lesser) counterpart must also be true. Paul, a trained rabbi, employed this principle in Romans 5:9. He argued that we may have confidence in our Savior as we anticipate Judgment Day because Jesus has already done the hard thing—He has justified us by His death on the cross. Since the greater thing is true ("justified by His blood"), the lesser must also be true ("saved . . . from the wrath of God"). The author of Hebrews used the same principle when he contrasted the sacrifices of the Mosaic Law with the sacrifice of Christ on the cross (Hebrews 9:13–14).

Hillel's second rule of interpretation might be described as "cut and paste" (*gezerah shavah*), where a passage from the Torah (Genesis through Deuteronomy, the Books of Moses) is illuminated and explained by a passage from the Prophets or the Writings (the three divisions of the Hebrew Scriptures are the Law, Prophets, and Writings). The passage from the Prophets or the Writings will contain the key word in the citation from the Law, helping the reader to understand its meaning and application. Paul used this rule of interpretation when he defended salvation by grace through faith alone in the promise of God to Abraham (Romans 4:1–8). Paul quoted Genesis 15:6 to prove that Abraham was saved by faith alone years before he was circumcised (Genesis 17): "For what does the Scripture say? 'Abraham believed God, and it was counted to him as righteousness'" (Romans 4:3). To clarify the meaning of *counted* ("reckoned, credited"), he then cited Psalm 32:1–2 (Romans 4:7–8), proving that *counted* denotes the forgiveness of sins apart from good works. This hermeneutical principle closely resembles "Scripture interprets Scripture," where we look at the clear passages to help illuminate and explain the difficult passages.

Whether trained in a rabbinical school or not, all New Testament authors see the Hebrew Scriptures Christologically, much as Jesus Himself did. That is, they interpret the Scriptures in view of the person and work of Jesus Christ for the sake of our salvation. When Jesus spoke in His hometown synagogue, He read Isaiah 61:1–2 and said "Today this Scripture has been fulfilled in your hearing" (Luke 4:21). When He walked with two downcast disciples on Easter Sunday afternoon, He lamented: "'O foolish ones, and slow of heart to believe all that the prophets have spoken! Was it not necessary that the Christ should suffer these things and enter into His glory?' And beginning with Moses and all the Prophets, He interpreted to them in all the Scriptures the things concerning Himself" (Luke 24:25–27).

We see the Gospel writers (especially Matthew) interpreting Hebrew Scriptures Christologically not only in direct prophecies but also indirectly, in events that on the surface don't seem like a prophecy at all. Matthew 2 serves to illustrate both of these uses.

When asked by Herod the Great (ruled 38–1 BC) where the Christ was to be born, the scribes (experts on the Hebrew Scriptures) told him "Bethlehem of Judea" (and then quoted Micah 5:2). This prophecy clearly identifies the little village of Bethlehem in Judea as the birthplace for the coming Messiah, a direct prophecy fulfilled by Jesus. (It is important especially for Matthew, who writes to a Jewish audience, that Jesus fulfills the prophecies concerning the messianic King.)

The next two Scripture passages cited by Matthew as prophecies don't seem to predict anything at all. The Holy Family travels to Egypt to avoid Herod's wrath and eventually returns to the Holy Land. Matthew notes: "This was to fulfill what the Lord had spoken by the prophet, 'Out of Egypt I called My son'" (Matthew 2:15, citing Hosea 11:1). In Hosea, the passage refers to the exodus (Exodus 12; 1446 BC) when God brought Israel (His "son") out of the land of slavery and death through the wilderness into the Promised Land.

Similarly, Matthew quotes Jeremiah 31:15 (in Matthew 2:18) and applies it to the slaughter of male infants in Bethlehem ordered by Herod the Great (Matthew 2:16). Matthew writes: "Then was fulfilled what was spoken by the prophet Jeremiah" (Matthew 2:17). In the original context of Jeremiah, the prophet portrays Rachel grieving for the captives as they are led from Jerusalem to Babylon in 587 BC. Since Rachel's grave is on this road near Ramah (Genesis 35:19), the prophet pictures her grieving over the death and exile of her descendants. How does this connect to the death of the children of Bethlehem in Jesus' day?

Both interpretations reflect a Christological reading of the Hebrew Scriptures. Israel, God's "son," often failed. In unbelief, they rebelled and perished. Jesus, God's Son, is Israel "rolled up into one." What Israel failed to do, Jesus accomplishes. In a sense, history repeats itself but has a dramatically different outcome. Whatever can be said about God's people in the Hebrew Scriptures finds its perfect fulfillment (repetition) in the person and work of Jesus Christ. In short, not only do the direct messianic prophecies of the Hebrew Scriptures find their fulfillment in Jesus of Nazareth, but the Old Testament as a whole comes to its completion in Him (see Luke 22:37; Acts 13:27; compare Paul's understanding of the Mosaic Law's purpose in Galatians 3:24–26).

The Early Church

Origen (AD 185–254) stands out as the best known biblical interpreter of the Early Church (from the first through the fourth centuries of our Lord). He spent most of his career in Alexandria, Egypt, and Caesarea, Palestine, teaching and writing extensively. Known as a philosopher and a theologian, he interpreted Holy Scripture allegorically and proposed three levels of meaning within each passage: a plain and obvious meaning, a moral meaning, and a spiritual meaning. Herbert Mayer, in his book *Interpreting the Holy Scriptures* (Concordia, 1967), offers the following example:

> One example of the allegorical method is his treatment of Joseph's many-colored coat. The first level of meaning, the "body" level (see 1 Thess. 5:23), was that Jacob made a special coat for his son. This was the only meaning that the majority of simple Christian Bible readers could see. But the second level, the "soul" level, was far more important. At this level the story contained a sharp moral warning against pride or favoritism. The third level, the mystical or "spiritual" level, however, was the most important. Here the coat stands for deep philosophical learning, and the 10 brothers are the evil men who want to drive all philosophy and learning out of the church. Only the best and wisest Christians, said Origen, could see the deepest or spiritual truth. (p. 25)

Allegory can be a helpful tool for illustrating an idea, as Paul used it in Galatians 4:21–31. However, it can easily be abused. Origen's allegorical approach allowed him to reinterpret any part of Scripture he found unacceptable or that clashed with his culture. It also made interpreting the Bible much easier. Instead of researching problem passages and resolving apparent conflicts within the text, the reader could simply make up his or her own interpretation and call that the "spiritual" or "deep" meaning of the passage. Holy Scripture is not potter's clay to be shaped and fashioned into whatever meaning the reader desires (see 2 Peter 1:19–21). The authors of Scripture had a message to convey and, moved by the Holy Spirit, produced the texts that have been recognized and read as God's Word. We might imagine that Origen's allegorical method received little acceptance in the Church, but it was very influential in the

Early Church and throughout the Middle Ages, up to the Reformation. For example, Ambrose of Milan (died AD 397) understood Scripture to communicate in more than one sense. He looked for a literal sense, a moral sense, and a spiritual (allegorical or mystical) sense. The allegorical approach even appears in modern pulpits, especially when preaching on the parables of Jesus. (How many times have we heard the Good Samaritan, Luke 10:25–37, allegorized—interpreting the Good Samaritan as Jesus, the man who fell among robbers as us, and the priest and Levite as the Mosaic Law?)

About the same time as the Alexandrian school of allegorical interpretation flourished (second through fourth centuries AD), a more conservative approach developed in Antioch of Syria (beginning in the third century AD). Stressing a literal interpretation of Scripture, this approach was reflected in the preaching and teaching of Theodore of Mopsuestia and St. John Chrysostom. Advocates of this way of reading Scripture stressed the historical context of Scripture and a careful evaluation of the grammar of God's Word. Although not as influential in the history of the Church as the Alexandrian school, it did attempt to stay grounded in Scripture.

Not only did different Christian schools of interpretation develop during these early centuries, but various semi-Christian religious systems flourished as well. Religious systems that denied the Trinity or the person of Christ in one form or another competed with orthodox Christian thought throughout the second through fifth centuries. Christian leaders met in councils to find ways to confess the faith that was faithful to Scripture (such as Nicaea in AD 325, Constantinople in AD 381, and Chalcedon in AD 451). Their statements of faith (creeds) reflect the consensus of Christians, spanning several centuries and many lands. These creeds formed the foundation of Christian tradition that continued to develop until the time of the Reformation.

The Medieval Church

Tradition played both a positive and a negative role throughout the Medieval Church. On the one hand, the creeds offered a "thumbnail sketch" of the Christian faith and could be used both to teach the faith as well as to identify false teachers. They still serve Christians this way today. If someone is looking for a church ("church shopping"), it is far more reliable to compare a church's teaching to the three Ecumenical

Creeds (Apostles', Nicene, and Athanasian) than to depend on the name of the church. Anyone can call himself a Christian or name their church "Christian," but a neglect or denial of the three great Ecumenical Creeds may reveal that they are not.

Negatively, tradition can too easily replace Scripture as the source and norm of all doctrine and practice. Jesus warned His followers about confusing the traditions of man and the commandments of God (Matthew 15:8–9). God's children should always check the Scriptures (as did the Bereans when Paul preached the Gospel to them, Acts 17:10–11). Human beings make mistakes, even popes and councils (as Martin Luther would point out).

We can depend only on Scripture for truth. Tradition serves as a "checks and balances" corrective for us as we read God's Word. As we saw earlier under the principle "rule of faith" in chapter 4, we read Holy Scripture both as individuals and as part of the Christian community. We read the Bible, a personal encounter with the living Word of God, and we develop an understanding of what a passage means. But we also want to compare our interpretation and understanding of Scripture with that of other believers as a kind of quality control, acknowledging our own limitations and distinctive perspective.

In the medieval era, interpreters were taught to seek four senses in each text of Scripture. However, in practice they were drawn most often to an allegorical interpretation, to the ultimate neglect of the literal sense. One can see this, for example, in so important a figure as Thomas Aquinas, who would later become the most influential theologian for Roman Catholicism. Interest in the literal sense of Scripture returned in the late medieval era through interpreters such as Nicholas of Lyra, who significantly influenced Martin Luther.

The Reformation

Although preceded by John Hus (died AD 1415), it fell to Martin Luther to bring Christians back to Scripture and make Scripture accessible to every believer. He translated the New Testament into the common language of the people (German) in AD 1522 and finished the entire Bible (including Apocrypha) by AD 1534. Nothing speaks more strongly of his convictions about Scripture than this translation, taking God's Word out of "protective custody" by the Church authorities and placing it in the hands of the individual Christian.

Luther believed the Bible to be the Word of God, the infallible and ultimate authority for the individual Christian as well as for the Church as a whole. No one and nothing superseded Scripture as the source and norm for doctrine and practice. His conviction was not the stuff of the ivory tower academic. He put his life on the line to defend it at the Diet of Worms (AD 1521) as did all who stood with him. (At that time, it was a capital offense to translate the Bible into the language of the people.)

Luther read the Scripture Christologically. He believed that the entire Bible pointed to Jesus Christ as Savior and Lord and that all the parts of Scripture revealed our need for a Savior and then led us to Him. Although he did not entirely abandon allegory, he emphasized the plain and simple meaning of the text as a primary principle for interpretation. The average Christian could therefore read and understand the Bible. Luther did not deny that some passages were difficult to understand, but he held fast to the conviction that the general meaning of Scripture is clear and obvious. Clear passages informed and illuminated the passages that were harder to understand (Scripture interprets Scripture).

Although Luther defended the right of each Christian to read and interpret the text on a "one-to-one" basis, he did not mean that everyone's personal interpretation is valid. He believed that Scripture contained an intended message and conveyed an objective truth. In other words, the person who reads the Bible and comes up with an interpretation can be totally wrong. Rather, Luther's point was this: just like the Bereans (Acts 17:10–12), it is our duty to read the Word and in its light evaluate the teachings of the Church. The high respect for the traditions of the Church can be demonstrated by remembering that the Confessions of the Lutheran Church begin with an unreserved subscription to the three Ecumenical Creeds (Apostles', Nicene, and Athanasian).

Many Protestant church bodies trace their lineage back to the French reformer John Calvin (AD 1509–64). He developed eight principles of interpretation for reading the Bible, closely resembling the approach (hermeneutics) of Martin Luther. Like Luther, Calvin believed there was only one intended meaning to the text and that was usually the plain and obvious meaning (the author wrote the text with one intended meaning in mind, *sensus literalis unus est*). Readers of later generations may apply that meaning differently according to their circumstances and interests, but there is only one objective meaning inherent in the written text.

He also challenged readers to approach the text with as few presuppositions as possible. We do not carefully read a text if we think that we know what it means before we begin. Only by prayer and the leading of the Holy Spirit (which Calvin argued was essential to interpreting God's Word) can we read carefully and grasp the intended meaning. An honest interpreter, such as Calvin, is always prepared to admit that he or she does not understand a text and to return to it later.

The Reformation times of Luther and Calvin saw a renewed appreciation for the Holy Scriptures as the true, inerrant, authoritative Word of God. The Bible possessed an inherent unity and served as the only reliable source for Christian doctrine. Only as led by the Holy Spirit could the believer read and understand the Scripture, which had Jesus Christ as its center and focus.

The remainder of the sixteenth and most of the seventeenth centuries might be described as a period of consolidation. The Roman Church responded to the Reformation with the Counter-Reformation, a revival especially of Thomas Aquinas's views that were codified by the Council of Trent (AD 1545–63). The core proclamation of the Reformers ("saved by grace through faith in Jesus Christ alone") was rejected at Trent, but the Roman Catholic Church did make a number of changes to address some of the issues of the Reformation. Both Lutherans (e.g., the Formula of Concord) and Roman Catholics (e.g., the Canons and Decrees of the Council of Trent) found ways to express their differing positions—often in a confrontational manner. As each side sought to defend its own positions and beliefs, biblical study was affected. This period has sometimes been called the period of "dead orthodoxy" because it seemed that eventually theologians neglected the Scripture and spent their time wrangling over relatively small doctrinal points.

Toward the end of the seventeenth century and into the eighteenth century, Pietism grew as a reaction against the problems of the previous period. Men like Philipp Spener (1635–1705), August Hermann Francke (1663–1727), and Johann Albrecht Bengel (1687–1752) emphasized the personal nature of a believer's relationship to God. Meeting in small groups, Pietists would study Scripture and encourage one another to put their faith into practice. Pietism generally encouraged lay leadership in the Church and stressed the practice of the faith over the confession of the faith (similar to Methodism in England). Herbert Mayer offers the following observation:

> The Pietists placed great emphasis upon the study of the original Biblical languages and upon the application of

> Scripture to daily life. Unfortunately, pietist hermeneutics also led to abuses. Some Pietists paid little attention to the discipline of hermeneutics and the original meaning of the passage. They frequently permitted their emotions to decide what the Spirit of God was saying. In some circles Pietists almost ignored the Bible in favor of their personal feelings and emotions. (*Interpreting the Holy Scriptures*, p. 30)

Modern Hermeneutics

Following the eras of Orthodoxy and Pietism, the so-called Age of Reason or Enlightenment swept Europe, bringing a new approach to science, philosophy, and—not surprisingly—religion. Philosophers like Baruch Spinoza (1632–77) and Voltaire (1694–1778), scientists such as Isaac Newton (1643–1727), and biblical critics such as the French priest Richard Simon (1638–1712) changed the Western European worldview. For rationalists, human reason transcended all other authority, including Scripture. So the historical-critical method was born.

The impact of the Enlightenment on Bible study had both positive and negative components. Positively, it reminded readers that Scripture has a human side. History (especially Israel's history), geography, and extrabiblical literature form the backdrop to the Holy Scriptures. Language, grammar, and syntax are all employed by the writers of the Bible to convey their message. The student of Scripture needs to have this in hand to read and understand God's Word.

Negatively, the Age of Reason denied the divine side of Scripture. Critics denied divine inspiration of the Word, rejected miracles, imagined errors and contradictions, and ridiculed those who remained faithful to the Scriptures. Failing to understand Scripture as a Middle-Eastern literary product, Western Europeans judged it by their own literary and scientific standards. It is no wonder they missed its message and misunderstood its nature.

In the nineteenth century, the Industrial Revolution made a major impact on Western society. Living standards rose for most people, and society seemed to improve at a rapid pace. Marxism proposed an evolution of society and economy through class struggle. Out of this class struggle in capitalism, a socialist society would emerge. Eventually the socialist society would evolve into a communist ideal—classless, stateless, and no private ownership. In the field of science, Charles Darwin (1809–82) imagined the same sort of evolution in biological terms. The struggle for existence would eventually result in the survival of the strongest (natural selection), which would then evolve. Life would continue to get better and better.

The same evolutionary concept impacted biblical studies as well. Hebert Mayer offers the following summary:

> They believed, for example, that the Christian religion was evolutionary and had moved from crude nature worship to advanced monotheism by the time of Isaiah and Micah. They dated complete books or, more commonly, portions of books by what they called the level of religious evolution that the contents represented. Julius Wellhausen (1844–1918) developed his theory of J, E, D, and P authors of parts of the Old Testament to support his evolutionary ideas. (*Interpreting the Holy Scriptures*, p. 31)

J, E, D, and P are abbreviations for theoretical authors—the J(Y)ahwist, Elohist, Deuteronomist, and Priestly authors—who wrote parts of the Books of Moses at different times over many centuries. Supporters of this theory look at Scripture through the lens of Western European thought, taking for granted the truth of their preconceived ideas (for example, that in a closed universe no miracles are possible). They offer more of a study in the exercise of a vivid imagination combined with cultural arrogance than any real help in reading the Bible with understanding.

From the twentieth century to the present, we see a broad diversity of hermeneutics that developed. The following list describes some key features of modern interpretation and its limitations.

Christological. First, many Christian interpreters, if not most, see Jesus of Nazareth as the center of Scripture. Opinions vary as to the nature of Christ and the significance of His person and work, but interpreters recognize that He sees Himself as the fulfiller of the Hebrew Scriptures and the promised Messiah of God.

Historical-Critical Method. This approach to reading Scripture seeks to discover the history behind the text. Those who read the Bible using this approach try to discover the original setting and shape of the text in order to discover the message of the author(s). The reader (or critic) sits above the text, peeling away layers of later addition until he or she discovers the earliest material. We see in the historical-critical method some of the same cultural arrogance of earlier hermeneutics, allowing the reader to assume the role of judge over the Word of God. Source criticism, form criticism, redaction criticism, and reader-response theory are all different schools of biblical criticism that employ the historical-critical method, as does "salvation history" (German: *Heilsgeschichte*). This school of thought sees Scripture as a record of historical events that are all the work of God interacting with human beings for the purpose of salvation.

Existential. Following in the footsteps of philosophers such as Martin Heidegger (1889–1976), hermeneutics shifted from what can be known about something (in this case, the text and the message it conveys) to the experience of interacting with the text. Using this approach, the objective meaning of the text is less important than sharing the experience of the author who wrote the text through the reader's encounter with the text. Those who advocate an existential encounter with Scripture seem to say that the reader of Scripture doesn't really receive any new revelation from God, but rather expands his or her understanding of self. It isn't so much God speaking to us through His living Word, but us expanding our understanding of ourselves through authentic personal encounters with the text. At best, the written text may be considered a record of someone's existential encounter with God. As the reader encounters the text and experiences it, such an encounter within the reader might also take place. As this experience occurs, the text becomes the Word of God for the reader. Karl Barth (1886–1968), for example, taught that Christ Jesus is truly the self-expression of God. God uses human language (the Scripture) to bridge the gap between Himself and fallen creation. As the reader encounters Christ through the experience of Scripture, he or she encounters God in a profound, life-impacting personal moment. Others, such as Rudolf Bultmann (1884–1976), "de-mythologized" the Bible to make its message acceptable to modern readers. Rejecting everything in Scripture that clashed with twentieth century Western sensibilities, he argued that only faith in the Christian proclamation (*kerygma*) was necessary for salvation.

Ecumenical. The twentieth century could fairly be described as the "age of ecumenism." As the Western Church had splintered in the sixteenth century and Protestant denominations had multiplied in the years following, the twentieth century saw a broad-based, concerted effort to unite. For the sake of organizational unity, doctrinal differences based on divergent readings of Scripture became less important. Church bodies discovered new ways of expressing their faith using language that was ambiguous enough that those who disagreed with their interpretation could agree on a joint confession of faith. The movement produced the World Council of Churches in 1948, a global fellowship of hundreds of church bodies dedicated to working together for the common good (environmental justice, help for the poor, etc.). We might say that this movement was made possible by the change in hermeneutics in the eighteenth and nineteenth centuries. As church bodies adopted principles of biblical interpretation that denied the authority of Holy Scripture and shifted interpretation away from the objective meaning of the text to a subjective experience with the Word, previous doctrinal divisions seemed unimportant. Oscar Cullmann (1902–99), an avid supporter of the ecumenical movement, understood sacred history as a line from the beginning (Genesis) to the end (Revelation) with Jesus Christ as its midpoint. We can see both positive and negative elements in this way of reading Scripture. At this early stage in the twenty-first century, it seems that the ecumenical movement is losing vitality.

Historical-Grammatical Method. The last century also saw the development of a more balanced method of reading the Bible, called the historical-grammatical method. This approach to reading Scripture appreciates the history behind a passage but also accepts the Bible as God's Word, authoritative and reliable. If it may be said that the historical-critical reader sits above the text, judging it by reason, then it may also be said that the historical-grammatical reader submits to the text, using reason but allowing it to remain subordinate to God's Word. The reader who uses the historical-grammatical method respects Scripture and asks, "What was the original message of the author(s)?"

Conclusions

The Word of God did come to real people in concrete, historical situations. The better we understand the historical context of a text, the more likely we are to read and understand it as it was intended to be read and understood. We appreciate the historical part of the historical-critical method, of which *Heilsgeschichte* is a part. On the other hand, the subjectivism inherent in the "critical" part leads the reader away from the text and back to the self. Rejecting that Scripture is inerrant and inspired, the critic dispenses with the nuts and bolts of the passage and moves toward his or her own goal. Practitioners of the historical-critical method often spend more time arguing about the historical background of a passage than dealing honestly with the passage at hand.

In Genesis 3:1, the serpent in the Garden of Eden asked Eve, "Did God actually say, . . . ?" Doubting God's clear Word, Adam and Even then lost their life in the garden and entered a world of death and despair. Satan continues to try to move God's children away from Scripture and, as we have seen from a survey of hermeneutical principles over the last several centuries, has been successful. Too often, modern critics forget that we battle spiritual forces, not flesh and blood (Ephesians 6:12). If the enemy can dislodge us from the Word of God, then he has won.

Having surveyed the hermeneutical approaches over the last several centuries, perhaps we would do well to remember the serpent's question in the garden and the outcome of abandoning God's Word. Reading the Bible is not simply an academic exercise. It is a personal experience with the living God through contact with His Word, which also serves as the "sword of the Spirit" in our battle against the forces of evil in our world (Ephesians 6:17). Every time we pick up the Bible and open it, we open our ears to hear the voice of our Good Shepherd (see John 10:1–16, 27–29). Therefore we undertake the task of reading the Bible seriously but also joyfully, because He speaks words of hope and salvation to us.

Appendix One
A Checklist For Bible Study Preparation

The following are steps that we recommend when studying a text of Scripture.

Step 1. **Pray**. As we noted above, reading the Bible is not an academic exercise. Holy Scriptures differ from other literary works, encompassing both a human side and a divine side. Only as the Holy Spirit opens our eyes to see can we perceive the truths of Scripture, both in the cognitive realm and as a personal encounter with the living Word of God.

Step 2. **Read the passage**. If possible, read the passage in several different translations. (If you have access to the original and the ability to read it, begin with that.) If you don't have a variety of translations available in book form, go online. The Bible Gateway website (www.biblegateway.com) has a tremendous variety of translations available. Try to slow down when you are reading, imagining that you have never seen this text before. Attempt to put aside everything you know about the passage while you are reading. See it with fresh eyes, catching details you might have missed before. Ask questions as you are reading, such as "why?" and "what?" and "when?" Look for other places in Scripture where key words or phrases appear (patterns of usage).

Step 3. **Read the context**. Look at the material before and after the passage you are studying. Ask yourself why the author placed this passage where he did. Look for connections to the preceding material that led the author to connect the passage you are studying with the surrounding parts.

Step 4. **Review the book as a whole**. If you have a study Bible, check the beginning of the biblical book for information on who wrote it, to whom, when, and why. Look at the broad outline of the biblical book and see where your passage fits. Try to see the whole picture ("the forest") as you look at the passage under consideration ("the tree"). Like an internal combustion engine, each part has its own shape and identity. And just like an internal combustion engine, each individual part has a role to play in making the whole thing work. There's a reason for each and every part of Scripture and a reason why it is located where it appears in the biblical book.

Step 5. **Look for textual variants**. This is easier in the original, but sometimes textual variants are included in translations as footnotes to the text. Are any of these variants significant? That is, do they affect the meaning of the passage?

Step 6. **Compare parallel accounts**. The Gospels (especially Matthew, Mark, and Luke) often record the same story, but each has its own personality. The Holy Spirit did not suppress the individuality of the people who wrote the Bible. Unlike demon possession (where the real person all but disappears), the Holy Spirit brought the whole person to the task of writing Scripture. Can you figure out why the author of the text you are studying wrote it the way he did? If you are in the Old Testament, you can do similar comparisons between some of the books (like Kings and Chronicles). If your text contains quotations or references to another biblical book (many New Testament works do), take the time to look up the reference or allusion. See what other authors do with the same text. For example, both Paul and the author of Hebrews quote Habakkuk 2:4 (see Romans 1:17; Galatians 3:11; Hebrews 10:38). If you have the time, do the detective work and track it down.

Step 7. **Check the historical and geographical references**. If your text mentions a person, place, or thing that is new to you, look it up. The Internet (if you have access to it) can serve you well when looking for information that the original readers (or hearers) of the text knew well. Along with the Bible study tools mentioned in chapter 12, pay attention to new books as they are published. Your local Christian bookstore or some of the online retailers (like Christian Book Distributors, www.christianbook.com) can be great places to check for new materials.

Step 8. **Talk with other Christians**. Whether in a group or one-on-one, other Christians can be a great resource as you read and consider a passage. Take advantage of their perspectives and life experiences. Reading the Bible is fundamentally an individual experience, but it also encompasses the community of believers. As Moses directs us, God wants us to talk about His Word with family and friends (Deuteronomy 6:7).

Step 9. **Determine the original point of the passage**. What did the author or speaker have in mind? What message did he want to communicate to his readers or hearers? Be sure to compare your results with the big picture of Scripture (the analogy of faith). If your understanding of the passage you are studying contradicts something in the historic creeds that Christians have used from ancient times, question your conclusions and go back to the drawing board to begin considering the passage again.

Step 10. **Apply the message**. How does the original meaning and point of the passage impact you and other Christians today? What direction does it provide you in your discipleship? What does the passage teach you about values and goals? In short, what does it mean for your faith and your life? This is where distinguishing the Law and the Gospel, sin and grace, of the passage is so helpful.

Appendix Two
A Biblical Chronology

Calculations based on the biblical record make it possible to date many events and the lives of people who participated in those events. Biblical history did not merely occur "once upon a time" as storytellers say. Biblical and Christian religion is historical, since God's supernatural revelation entered ordinary space and time.

Stone Age culture shows some evidence of record keeping. (See the interesting overview of research in Richard Rudgley, *The Lost Civilizations of the Stone Age* [New York: The Free Press, 1999].) However, historians and archaeologists typically date the development of writing as we know and use it today to the end of the fourth millennium BC and associate early writing with Mesopotamia and Egypt. The genealogies of Genesis 5; 10–11 are perhaps incomplete, so historians cannot effectively calculate dates from them. (The geneological lists in Genesis 5 and 11 each contain exactly ten generations, suggesting that they are arranged for effect.) The first dateable person in the Bible is Abram (Abraham), who was born in Mesopotamia near the end of the third millennium BC and later traveled to Egypt (Genesis 12).

Calculating Dates

The following chronology allows the reader to compare the biblical record of events with parallel records of events in world history, with special attention to the civilizations that most often interacted with the people of Israel. Users should be aware that scholars of history may differ considerably when dating specific kings and events (e.g., dates proposed for the early dynasties of Egypt often differ by as much as fifty years). Although historians may fix some dates on the basis of astronomical events described in ancient texts, they estimate most dates by comparing lists of kings and events.

Historians sometimes have difficulty determining the dates for biblical persons and events after Abram. (E.g., dates for the exodus and conquest are hotly debated in academic circles.) Dating usually grows easier and clearer as one moves forward in history. (E.g., for Israel, dates from the kingdom period and forward are more easily calculated.) Bracketed notes represent a proposed construction based on biblical and historical contexts.

EVENTS FROM CREATION TO THE FLOOD	
BIBLICAL RECORD	RECORDS OF OTHER CIVILIZATIONS
Creation in six days (Gn 1–2)	Creation accounts in Mesopotamia and other cultures have similarities with biblical themes but differ markedly in theology.
Fall into sin (Gn 3)	
Children of Adam and Eve (Gn 4–5; 10). Moses may refer to an earlier resource for his information: The Book of the Generations of Adam.	
Noah called to build the ark (Gn 6) The flood (Gn 7–8) God's promise to Noah (Gn 9)	Flood accounts in various world cultures describe a great worldwide flood during which a hero rescues animals and mankind (e.g., Sumerian Kings List, Atrahasis Epic, Eridu Flood Story, and Epic of Gilgamesh). Such flood accounts are not limited to Mesopotamia.
The tower of Babel (Gn 11)	The Sumerian Epic of Enmerkar refers to a common language spoken by all people.

Although writing began at an earlier date (e.g., Sumerian records of commerce may date to c 3300 BC), recorded history began when the Egyptians used hieroglyphs to describe the unification of Upper and Lower Egypt under Menes in c 3100 BC. After this point, it becomes possible to calculate dates for persons and events, though many difficulties still result because of the variety of calendars, writing systems, and styles used by ancient people.

DATEABLE, RECORDED HISTORY				
Anatolia, Greece, and Rome	Egypt and Africa	Dates	Syria, Canaan, and Israel	Mesopotamia and Persia
	Menes unites Upper and Lower Egypt; 1st Egyptian Dynasty	c 3100 BC	Gebal/Byblos serves as an important trade center with Egypt; Jericho is a long-established city	
	2nd Dynasty begins	2890	Temple gifts at Gebal/Byblos bear the name of Egyptian ruler Khasekhemui	
		c 2700		Sumerian royal inscriptions begin; early dynasty of Sumerians emerging; name of ruler Enmebaragesi found in archaeological remains from this time

Anatolia, Greece, and Rome	Egypt and Africa	Dates	Syria, Canaan, and Israel	Mesopotamia and Persia
	Djoser reigns; 3rd Dynasty; Imhotep builds step pyramid	2686		
		c 2500		Writings in Mari
	5th Dynasty	c 2494		
		c 2400		Writings in Assyria
	6th Dynasty	c 2345		
		c 2334	Sargon conquers Syrian states; they yield various goods to him	Sargon I of Akkad; followed by Akkadian Dynasty
		c 2290–2250	Ebla flourishes as trade center between Mediterranean region and Mesopotamia	

THE PATRIARCHS OF ISRAEL

Anatolia, Greece, and Rome	Egypt and Africa	Dates	Syria, Canaan, and Israel	Mesopotamia and Persia
		2166 BC		Abram born (Gn 11:27–32)
	Intermediate period; invaders divide and disrupt Egypt	c 2160–2040		
		c 2150		Gutians invade and disrupt Ur
		c 2156		Sarai born (Gn 17:17)
		c 2112–c 2095		Ur-Nammu, founder of the 3rd Sumerian Dynasty of Ur and the Sumerian legal code, builds step pyramid
		c 2100	Amorite invasion destroys Gebal/Byblos	
		2091		Abram moves from Haran to Canaan (Gn 12:4)
		2067	Abram given the name Abraham, circumcised with Ishmael (Gn 17:1–6, 24–25)	
	Egyptian Middle Kingdom	c 2040–1786		
		c 2030	Sarah dies (Gn 23:1–2)	
		2026	Isaac marries Rebekah (Gn 25:20)	

Anatolia, Greece, and Rome	Egypt and Africa	Dates	Syria, Canaan, and Israel	Mesopotamia and Persia
		2006	Jacob and Esau born (Gn 25:24–26)	
		2004		Dynasty of Ur-Nammu ends
Minoan culture builds palaces on Crete		c 2000	Pottery imported from Cyprus reaches Canaan	
	Mentuhotep unites Egypt; 12th Dynasty begins with powerful pharaohs	1991	Abraham dies (Gn 25:7)	
		1966	Esau marries Judith (Gn 26:34)	
		1943	Ishmael dies (Gn 25:17)	
Hittites emerging in Anatolia; Greek pottery uses hieroglyphic script		c 1900		
	[Joseph sold into slavery in Egypt (Gn 37:2, 12–28)]	inter 1901–1897		
		1894		Sumuabum establishes Amorite Dynasty at Babylon
		1886	Isaac dies (Gn 35:28–29)	
	[Joseph enters service in Pharaoh's court (Gn 41:46)]	inter 1888–1884		
	Jacob goes to Egypt (Apr; Gn 47:9, 28; Ex 12:40–41)	1876		
	Jacob dies (Gn 47:28)	1859		
		c 1830		Iakhdunlim strengthens Mari
	[Joseph dies (Gn 50:22, 26)]	inter 1808–1804		Assyrians build temple to Sumerian god Enlil

ISRAEL IN EGYPT

Anatolia, Greece, and Rome	Egypt and Africa	Dates	Syria, Canaan, and Israel	Mesopotamia and Persia
Linear A script at Crete		c 1800–1450 BC		Hurrians spreading influence
		1792–1750		Hammurabi of Babylon
	2nd Intermediate Period	1786–1567		
		c 1775	Aleppo, an important trade center under the ruler Iarimlim	Mari flourishes as a trade center, as recorded in the archives of Alalakh
		1756		Hammurabi destroys Mari
	Hyksos invade and dominate Egypt	c 1750		
Labarnas founds Hittite Empire		c 1680		
		c 1670		Ashur (Akkadian/Assyrian) Dynasty emerges
Hattusilis I expands Hittite Empire	17th Dynasty established at Thebes	c 1650	N. Syria falls to the Hittites	Kassite Dynasty emerges in Babylon
Mursilis I leads Hittites to victory over Aleppo and Babylon		c 1590	Aleppo defeated	Hittites defeat Amorite Dynasty of Babylon
	Hyksos expelled	c 1580 1570		
	Ahmose begins New Kingdom; 18th Dynasty	c 1570	Fleeing Hyksos occupy Sharuhen, Egyptians destroy the city	
Telipinus issues edict regulating Hittite succession and courts		1530		
	Moses born (Ex 7:7; Dt 34:7); Thutmose I claims Syria	1526		
Mycenaeans trade with Canaanites		c 1500	Mycenaean designs influence Canaanites	Mitanni Empire emerges in N. Mesopotamia under Saustatar
	Amenhotep II quells rebellion in Orontes Valley	1488	Cities of the Orontes Valley revolt against Egyptian rule	

THE EXODUS AND THE CONQUEST

Anatolia, Greece, and Rome	Egypt and Africa	Dates	Syria, Canaan, and Israel	Mesopotamia and Persia
	Thutmose III destroys coalition at Megiddo	c 1468 BC	Canaanite Prince of Kadesh coalition defeated	
	Thutmose III co-regent with Amenhotep II, who campaigns in Asia	c 1450		
Destruction of Greek palaces (e.g., Knossos)	1st Passover; exodus (Apr; Ex 12:6; 1Ki 6:1; Nu 33:3)	1446	Passover in Sinai (Apr; Nu 9:1); Israel arrives at Wilderness of Sin (May; Ex 16:1) and Wilderness of Sinai (May/June; Ex 19:1)	
		1445	Tabernacle set up (Mar/Apr; Ex 40:2,17); census taken (Apr/May; Nu 1:1–2, 18); Israel leaves Wilderness of Sinai (May; Nu 10:11)	
		1444	Israel leaves Kadesh (Dt 2:14)	
	Thutmose IV makes peace with Mitanni Empire; Amarna Letters	c 1425		Mitanni and Egyptians cease long struggle over Syria
		1407	Israel arrives at Wilderness of Zin (Apr/May; Nu 20:1); Aaron dies (July/Aug; Nu 33:38)	
		1407/1406	Moses addresses Israel (Dec/Jan; Dt 1:3)	
		1406	Israel crosses the Jordan (Apr; Jsh 4:19); 1st Passover in the land (Jsh 5:10)	
Hittite New Kingdom emerges		1400	Joshua gives Hebron to Caleb (Jsh 14:10)	
		1399–1375	Death of Joshua and the elders (Jgs 2:6–10)	

THE JUDGES OF ISRAEL

Anatolia, Greece, and Rome	Egypt and Africa	Dates	Syria, Canaan, and Israel	Mesopotamia and Persia
	Akhenaton (Amenhotep IV) introduces monotheistic religious reforms	c 1379 BC	Judges lead Israel c 300 years	
Hittite expansion under Suppiluliumus I		c 1375	Hittites retake Syria	
Hittites defeat Mitanni		c 1360	Cities of Syria ally with Mitanni and suffer defeat from the Hittites	Hittites and Ashur-uballit I defeat Mitanni ruler Tushratta; Mitanni becomes part of Hittite Empire
	Ramses I begins 19th Dynasty	1332	Eglon oppresses Israel	
		c 1307–1275		Adad-nirari I of Assyria defeats Kassites and Mitanni
Battle of Kadesh between Hittites and Egyptians	Ramses II defeated at Kadesh	1286		
Troy violently destroyed		c 1275		Shalmaneser I defeats Mitanni; builds 2nd capital at Calah
		1236	Jabin oppresses Israel	
		1234		Tukulti-ninurta I defeats Kassite Dynasty of Babylon; however, Kassites regain control
	Sea Peoples invade Egypt	1230		
Hattusus burned; Hittite Empire collapses	Senakht begins 20th Dynasty	c 1200		
Sea Peoples (Philistines?) invade coast of Canaan	Egyptian influence diminished	1190	Philistine cities emerging in Gaza	
		1124–1103		Nebuchadrezzar I (Assyrian) makes Babylon his capital
		c 1114–c 1076		Tiglath-pileser I of Assyria expands empire and wins victories against Babylon

Anatolia, Greece, and Rome	Egypt and Africa	Dates	Syria, Canaan, and Israel	Mesopotamia and Persia
	21st Dynasty (Tanite); Egyptian weakness	1085		
		1099–1060	Eli, priest and judge (1Sm 4:15, 18)	
		1060	Ark in Philistine territory (1Sm 6:1)	

THE KINGDOM OF ISRAEL

Anatolia, Greece, and Rome	Egypt and Africa	Dates	Syria, Canaan, and Israel	Mesopotamia and Persia
Collapse of Mycenaean culture; Linear B script no longer used		c 1050 BC		
		1048–1009	Saul reigns over Israel (1Sm 13:1; Ac 13:21)	
		1039	David born (2Sm 5:1–5)	
		1010–1009	David lives in Philistine territory (1Sm 27:7)	
		1009–970	David reigns seven years in Hebron, then over all Israel in Jerusalem (2Sm 5:5; 1Ki 2:11)	
	Pharaoh's daughter marries Solomon	970–931	Reign of Solomon (1Ki 12:42)	
		967–960	Temple built and dedicated (1Ki 6:1; 2Ch 3:1–2; 2Ch 7:7–10)	

THE DIVIDED KINGDOMS: ISRAEL AND JUDAH

Anatolia, Greece, and Rome	Egypt and Africa	Dates	Syria, Canaan, and Israel	Mesopotamia and Persia
	Shoshenq I founds 22nd Dynasty	945 BC		

Anatolia, Greece, and Rome	Egypt and Africa	Dates	Syria, Canaan, and Israel	Mesopotamia and Persia
		931	Israel divided under Rehoboam	
		927	Shishak (Shoshenq I) invades Israel (1Ki 14:25; 2Ch 12:2)	Ashur-dan II revives Assyria
Phoenician temple built on Crete; Etruscans emerging in Italy		c 900		
		898	Asa's reform/covenant (May/June; 2Ch 15:10–12)	
		883–859		Ashurnasirpal II of Assyria expands his empire, slaughtering prisoners and deporting conquered people
		871	Jehoshaphat sends teachers throughout Israel (2Ch 17:7)	
		858–824	N. Syria falls to Shalmaneser; Damascus besieged	Shalmaneser III of Assyria
		855–853	No war between Israel and the Arameans (1Ki 22:1)	
		853	Battle of Qarqar between Aramean kings and Assyrians	
		841–835	Athaliah rules Judah; Joash hidden in temple	
		c 828–824		Rebellion complicates Assyrian succession; Shamshi-Adad emerges as ruler with help of Babylonians
	23rd Dynasty begins	817		
	Tyrians found Carthage	c 813	Jerusalem temple repaired (2Ki 12:6–7)	
		804	Damascus conquered	Adad-nirari III of Assyria takes over Syria
Etruscan city-states emerge in central Italy		c 800		
		c 783–773		Shalmaneser IV of Assyria

Anatolia, Greece, and Rome	Egypt and Africa	Dates	Syria, Canaan, and Israel	Mesopotamia and Persia
1st Olympiad		775	Jotham born (2Ki 15:32–33; 2Ch 27:1)	
		773	Shalmaneser IV leads unsuccessful campaign against Damascus	
		744–727		Tiglath-pileser III of Assyria
		740	Hezekiah born (2Ki 18:1–2; 2Ch 29:1); Isaiah's vision (Is 6)	
Greeks colonize locations around the Mediterranean		c 734–580		
		724–722	Samaria besieged (2Ki 18:9–10)	

ISRAEL IN EXILE

Anatolia, Greece, and Rome	Egypt and Africa	Dates	Syria, Canaan, and Israel	Mesopotamia and Persia
		722 BC	Fall of Samaria to Assyrians	
		721–705		Sargon II of Assyria
	25th Dynasty of Shabaka (Cushite)	716		
		715	Hezekiah repairs temple (2Ch 29:3; Is 14:28–32)	
		704–681		Sennacherib of Assyria
		c 701	Sennacherib besieges Jerusalem (2Ki 18:13; Is 36:1); Hezekiah's sickness; Hezekiah pays tribute to Sennacherib	
Carchemish preserves Hittite script and culture to this point		700		
	Assyrians occupy Egypt	671		Esarhaddon takes Egypt; height of Assyrian Empire
		668–c 627		Ashurbanipal, last great ruler of Assyria

Anatolia, Greece, and Rome	Egypt and Africa	Dates	Syria, Canaan, and Israel	Mesopotamia and Persia
	26th Dynasty begins; Psamtik expels Assyrians	664–663		
2nd Messenian War		650		
		633	Jehoiakim born (2Ki 23:36; 2Ch 36:5); Josiah seeks the Lord	
Cylon attempts coup in Athens		c 630		
		629	Josiah purges high places (2Ch 34:3)	
		628	Jeremiah called to be a prophet (Jer 1:1–2)	
		625–605		Nabopolassar of Neo-Babylonia
		623	Book of the Law found in the temple; Josiah's Passover (Apr 15; 2Ch 35:1, 19)	
Etruscan Dynasty of Tarquius begins		616	Jehoiachin born (2Ki 24:8; 2Ch 36:9)	
		c 612–609		Chaldeans and Medes destroy Assyrian rule
	Pharaoh Neco defeated at Carchemish	605	Nebuchadnezzar besieges Jerusalem (2Ki 24:1); Judeans first removed from Judah (Jer 24, 36, 45–46; Dn 1)	
		604–562		Nebuchadnezzar of Neo-Babylonia
		604	Fast proclaimed; Baruch reads scroll (inter Nov 24–Dec 23; Jer 36:9–10, 22)	
	Egyptians repel Babylonians	601	Jehoiakim rebels against Nebuchadnezzar	Babylonians turned back near Gaza
Phocaea Greeks colonize Spain		600		
		599	Nebuchadnezzar takes captives (Jer 52:28)	
		597	Nebuchadnezzar besieges Jerusalem (2Ki 24:10; 2Ch 36:10)	

Anatolia, Greece, and Rome	Egypt and Africa	Dates	Syria, Canaan, and Israel	Mesopotamia and Persia
Solon's reforms in Athens		594	Hananiah confronts Jeremiah (Jer 28:1); Hananiah dies (Jer 28:17)	
		593		Ezekiel's 1st vision (July 31; Ezk 1:1–2)
		589	Siege of Jerusalem (Jer 32:1–2; 39:1; 52:4; Ezk 24–25)	
		587	Final siege of Jerusalem begins (2Ki 25:1; Ezk 24:1–2)	Oracles against Egypt (Ezk 29:1–2) and Pharaoh (Ezk 30:20–22; 31:1–2)

JUDAH IN EXILE

Anatolia, Greece, and Rome	Egypt and Africa	Dates	Syria, Canaan, and Israel	Mesopotamia and Persia
		587 BC	Wall of Jerusalem breached (July 29; 2Ki 25:3–4; Jer 39:2; 52:6–7); Nebuzaradan burns the temple (Aug 28; Jer 52:12–13); Gedaliah killed (2Ki 25:25; Jer 41:1–2)	
		573		Ezekiel's vision of a new Jerusalem (Ezk 40–48)
		inter 573–569		Nebuchadnezzar's 2nd dream and humiliation (Dn 4)
Croesus of Lydia		561		Evil-merodach of Neo-Babylonia; Jehoiachin freed from prison (2Ki 25:27; Jer 52:31)
Homer's poems set down in writing		c 560		Nergal Shar Usur of Neo-Babylonia
		559–529		Rise of Persian Empire under Cyrus II
		553		Ancient of Days vision (Dn 7)
Cyrus defeats Lydians; Persian pressure drives Phocaeans west to Italy and Spain		551		Goat and ram vision (Dn 8); Cyrus II of Persia defeats Croesus of Lydia; Ionian Greeks become Persian subjects

JUDEANS RETURN FROM EXILE

Anatolia, Greece, and Rome	Egypt and Africa	Dates	Syria, Canaan, and Israel	Mesopotamia and Persia
		538 BC		Cyrus rules Babylon; Cyrus's decree (Ezr 1:1; 5:13; 6:3)
		537	Altar in Jerusalem rebuilt (Ezr 3)	
		536	2nd temple begun (inter Apr 29–May 28; Ezr 3:8)	Daniel in mourning; prince of Persia opposes angel (Apr 3–23; Dn 10:2, 13)
Greeks attempt westward expansion	Carthage and Etruscans halt Greek expansion	c 535		
		530	Work on temple halted (Ezr 4:24)	
	Achaemenid 27th Dynasty under Cambyses	525		Cambyses II of Persia (528–523 BC)
		522–486		Darius I of Persia
		520	Messages of Haggai and Zechariah (Hg 1–2; Zec 1)	
		516	2nd temple finished (Feb 21; Ezr 6:15)	Darius campaigns against Scythians
Roman republic founded		509		
Cleisthenes reforms Athenian constitution toward democracy	Carthage concludes peace treaty with Rome	c 508		
Ionian revolt against Persia		499		Persians mobilize against Ionian tyrants
Battle of Marathon; Greeks defeat Persians		490		Darius defeated at Marathon
		486	Letter written to Xerxes (Ezr 4:6)	
Greeks defeat Persians at Thermopylae, Artemisium, Salamis		480		Greeks defeat huge Persian force
		478		Xerxes of Persia marries Esther (Est 2:16–17)

Anatolia, Greece, and Rome	Egypt and Africa	Dates	Syria, Canaan, and Israel	Mesopotamia and Persia
		474		Haman issues edict about Jews (Apr 17; Est 3:12); Mordecai issues counter-edict (July 23; Est 8:9)
		464–424		Artaxerxes I of Persia
1st Peloponnesian War		460–446		
Athenians support Inaros's revolt	Lybian Prince Inaros revolts against Persians	459		
		458	Ezra arrives in Jerusalem (Oct 31; Ezr 7:8–9)	Ezra leaves Babylon (Apr 8; Ezr 7:9); Ezra leaves Ahava River (Apr 19; Ezr 8:31)
	Herodotus in Egypt	c 450		
Athens makes peace with Persia		449		
Canuleian Law (Roman)		445	Walls of Jerusalem completed (Oct 3; Ne 6:15); Nehemiah holds convocation (Oct 8; Ne 7:73; 8:2)	Nehemiah requests leave to go to Jerusalem (inter Apr 13–May 11; Ne 2:1–5)
		433/432		Nehemiah returns to Susa (Ne 13:6)
Great Peloponnesian War		431–404		

THE TIME BETWEEN THE TESTAMENTS

Anatolia, Greece, and Rome	Egypt and Africa	Dates	Syria, Canaan, and Israel	Mesopotamia and Persia
		423–405 BC		Darius II of Persia
	Priests of Khnum and Persians destroy Jewish temple in Egypt	410		
	Amyrtaeus rebels, establishes Saite 28th Dynasty	c 405		

Anatolia, Greece, and Rome	Egypt and Africa	Dates	Syria, Canaan, and Israel	Mesopotamia and Persia
Pelopon-nesian War ends		404		
		404–359/358		Artaxerxes II of Persia
Gauls capture Rome		390		
	30th Dynasty	380		
Philip II of Macedon		359–336		
		358–338		Artaxerxes III of Persia
	Carthage concludes treaty with Rome	348		
1st Samnite War begins; Roman power expands	31st Dynasty under Artaxerx-es III	343		Persians attack at Pelusium
Rome wins Latin War		341		
Dissolution of Latin League		338		Artaxerxes III murdered; Arses (Xerxes II) rules Persia
Alexander rules Mace-donia		336		
	Darius III takes Egypt	335		Darius III rules Persia until 331
Alexander de-feats Persians at Issus		333		
	Alexander pro-claimed pharaoh	332	Alexander takes Judea away from Persians	
Alexander the Great dies at Babylon		323		
	Ptolemy I founds Ptole-maic Dynasty (Greek)	305		Seleucus I Nicator founds Seleucid Dynasty (Greek)
1st Punic War; Roman power expands	Carthaginians lose territory to Rome	264–241		
2nd Punic War		218–202		
	Ptolemy IV defeats Antio-chus III	217	Battle of Raphia secures Ptolemaic rule of Judea	Antiochus III defeated at Raphia

Anatolia, Greece, and Rome	Egypt and Africa	Dates	Syria, Canaan, and Israel	Mesopotamia and Persia
	Scopus defeated; Ptolemies lose Judea, make peace with Seleucids	198	Battle of Panias; Jews in Egypt and Judea are separated from one another politically	Antiochus III takes over Judea
Romans defeat Antiochus III at Smyrna		190		Antiochus III loses much of Asia Minor to Rome, faces financial trouble
		174	Jason bribes Antiochus III to secure the high priesthood at the Jerusalem temple	
		171	Menelaus, a non-Levite, purchases the priesthood at Jerusalem; Jason removed	
		c 168	Mattathias dies	
Romans conquer Macedonia	Antiochus IV Epiphanes engaged in war with Egypt	167	Antiochus IV orders pigs to be sacrificed to Olympian Zeus at the Jerusalem temple, leading to the Maccabean revolt; sacrilege continues for 2½ years	Antiochus IV Epiphanes forces Syrian laws on Judeans
		166	Battle of Beth-horon	
		165	Judas Maccabeus leads rebellion against Seleucids	
		164	Maccabees retake and purify Jerusalem; Hanukkah established	
		153	Jonathan officiates as high priest at Feast of Booths	Syrian conflict between Demetrius I and Alexander Balas; Seleucid Kingdom declines; knowledge of cuneiform script is lost
		147	Battle of Jamnia	
3rd Punic War; Romans destroy Corinth	Romans destroy Carthage	146		
	Infighting divides Ptolemies	145		
		141	Simon takes Akra, enters Jerusalem	Parthians begin to take over Mesopotamia
		135	Ptolemy murders Simon, last son of Mattathias; John Hyrcanus accepts Syrian rule	Antiochus VII Sidetes besieges Jerusalem

Anatolia, Greece, and Rome	Egypt and Africa	Dates	Syria, Canaan, and Israel	Mesopotamia and Persia
		104–103	Aristobulus rules	
		103–76	Alexander Jannaeus rules	
		76–67	Alexandra rules	
Romans fight slave war with Spartacus		73–71		
		67–63	Aristobulus II rules	
Romans establish Idumean Dynasty under Antipater		63	Idumean Dynasty under Antipater	
Caesar's Gallic Wars		59–51		
Crassus defeated at Carrhae		53		Battle of Carrhae; Parthians defeat Romans
	Cleopatra VII and Ptolemy XIII enthroned	52		
Julius Caesar crosses the Rubicon and becomes Roman dictator		49–44		
	Cleopatra's son Caesarion born	47	Herod made tetrarch of Galilee	
Caesar assassinated		44		
		43	Malchus poisons Antipater	
Octavian (Augustus) and Antony defeat Cassius and Brutus at Philippi		42	Herod the Great and Phasael made tetrarchs of Judea	
Octavian appoints Herod ruler of Judea		40	Herod flees from Parthians to Rome, returns as ruler	Parthians invade Judea but later withdraw
Battle of Actium; Egyptians withdraw	Egyptians claim victory at Actium	31		
Rome rules Egypt until AD 642	Antony and Cleopatra commit suicide	30		

Anatolia, Greece, and Rome	Egypt and Africa	Dates	Syria, Canaan, and Israel	Mesopotamia and Persia
Augustus, 1st Roman emperor		27 BC–AD 14		
		14–4 BC	Family feuds trouble Herod	

THE NEW TESTAMENT

Anatolia, Greece, and Rome	Egypt and Africa	Dates	Syria, Canaan, and Israel	Mesopotamia and Persia
		4 BC	Angel appears to Zechariah (c Nov 15; Lk 1:8–22)	
		3 BC	The annunciation (inter Apr 17–May 16; Lk 1:26–38); John the Baptist born (Aug; Lk 1:57–66)	
	Holy family in Egypt	2 BC	Jesus born (mid Jan to early Feb; Mt 1:25; Lk 2:1–7); Magi visit; flight to Egypt (mid to late in the year; Mt 2)	
		1 BC	Death of Herod the Great (after Jan 10; Mt 2:19); return to Nazareth (Mt 2:19–23)	
		AD 6	Judas the Galilean leads revolt against Rome; Judea, Samaria, and Idumaea combined to form the Roman province of Judea	
		c 10	Rabbi Hillel dies	
		11	Jesus in temple before the elders (c Apr 8–22; Lk 2:42)	
Tiberius, Roman emperor		14–37		
Revolt in Gaul; grain shortages cause unrest in Rome		21		
		29	Baptism of Jesus (Fall; Lk 3:1–2)	
		30	Jesus at Passover (c Apr 8; Jn 2:20)	

Anatolia, Greece, and Rome	Egypt and Africa	Dates	Syria, Canaan, and Israel	Mesopotamia and Persia
		32	Jesus at Passover (c Apr 15; Jn 6:4); Jesus arrives at Feast of Booths (c Oct 14; Jn 7:14); Feast of Booths (Oct 17 or 18; Jn 7:37)	
Roman Senators unable to pay debts; subsidized by Emperor Tiberius		33	Triumphal entry (Sun, Mar 29); Last Supper (Thurs eve, Apr 2); crucifixion (Fri, Apr 3); resurrection (Sun, Apr 5); ascension (May 14; Lk 24:51; Ac 1:9); Pentecost (May 24)	Jews of Parthia, Media, Elam, and Mesopotamia travel to Jerusalem for Pentecost
	Ethopian eunuch baptized, returns home (Ac 8:26–39)	35-42		Revolt of Seleucia on the Tigris against Parthian Rule
		36	Paul's conversion (Ac 9:1–31)	
Caligula (Gaius), Roman emperor		37–41	Josephus, Jewish historian, born	
	Philo of Alexandria leads Jewish delegation to Rome	c 39	Caligula attempts to place statue of himself in Jerusalem temple	
		41	Martyrdom of James (late Mar; Ac 12:2); Peter in prison (Apr; Ac 12:3–4); Passover (May 4; Ac 12:4); Peter leaves Jerusalem (May; Gal 2:11)	
		41–44	Herod Agrippa I rules Judea	
Claudius, Roman emperor		41–54		
Peter on mission in Asia Minor (Spr/Sum; 1Pt 1:1–2); [in Corinth (Fall); at Rome (mid Nov)]		42	Peter in Antioch (May 41–Apr 42; Gal 2:11)	
		44	Herod Agrippa at festival in Caesarea (Mar 5; Ac 12:19); death of Herod Agrippa (Mar 10; Ac 12:21–23)	

Anatolia, Greece, and Rome	Egypt and Africa	Dates	Syria, Canaan, and Israel	Mesopotamia and Persia
		47–48	Paul's 1st missionary journey (Ac 13:1–14:28)	
Paul goes to Macedonia; Barnabas and John Mark go to Cyprus (mid May; Ac 15:36–16:10)		49	Conference in Jerusalem (Ac 15:1–35); Peter goes to Antioch (Feb; Gal 2:11); Paul confronts Peter (Apr; Gal 2:11)	
Paul's 2nd missionary journey (Ac 15:39–18:22)	Philo of Alexandria leads second Jewish delegation to Rome	49–51		
		49–56	[Peter in Antioch (seven years)]	
Paul's 3rd missionary journey (Ac 18:23–21:17)		52–55		
Nero, Roman emperor		54–68		
		55–57	Paul imprisoned in Caesarea (Ac 23:23–26:32)	
Paul's journey to Rome (Ac 27:1–28:16)		57–58		
Paul in custody in Rome (Ac 28:17–31)		58–60		
		62	Martyrdom of James, the Lord's brother	
Paul assigns Titus at Crete (Ti 1:5)		64–65		
Paul in Ephesus, where he leaves Timothy (Spr–Sum; 1Tm 1:3)		65		
	Tiberias Julius Alexander, of Jewish descent appointed Roman prefect of Egypt	66–70	Jewish revolt against Romans	

Anatolia, Greece, and Rome	Egypt and Africa	Dates	Syria, Canaan, and Israel	Mesopotamia and Persia
Peter and Paul martyred		68		
Emperor Vespasian		69–79		
		70	Titus destroys Jerusalem temple; Rabbon Yohanan ben Zakkai at Yavneh Academy	Jerusalem Jews settle in Babylonia, which becomes the new center of Judaism
		c 73	Fall of Masada	
Emperor Titus		79–81		
Emperor Domitian		81–96		
		c 90–115	Rabbon Gamaliel II at Yavneh Academy	
Jews revolt in Cyprus	Jews revolt in Egypt and Cyrene	115–17		Trajan captures Mesopotamia; Jews revolt
	Founding of Antinoöpolis by Emperor Hadrian	130		
		132–35	Bar Kokhba revolt; death of Rabbi Akiva, Yavneh Academy leader who hailed Bar Kokhba as the messiah	

Subject Index

Scripture Index

Old Testament

Genesis

Exodus

Leviticus

Numbers

Deuteronomy

John

Acts

Jude

Revelation